Our Lady of Champion: Prayer Book for Pilgrims

Our Lady of Champion: Prayer Book for Pilgrims

Fr. Edward Looney

TAN Books
Gastonia, North Carolina

Nihil Obstat: Very Reverend John W. Girotti, JCL

Imprimatur: Most Reverend David L. Ricken, DD, JCL

Cover design by Jordan Avery

Cover image: *Our Lady of Champion* by Gwyneth Thompson-Briggs, 2024. Located in the National Shrine of Our Lady of Champion, Wisconsin.

ISBN: 978-1-5051-3744-6

Published in the United States by
TAN Books
PO Box 269
Gastonia, NC 28053
www.TANBooks.com

Printed and Bound in the United States of America.

PRESENTED TO

Name

Date / Occasion

Personal Note

Contents

Part I

Introductory Essays Concerning Marian Apparitions and the Shrine of Our Lady of Champion

Private Revelation, Biblical and Historical. 3
Mary Visits Wisconsin 10
Analyzing the Apparition. 26
Method of Approval for Marian Apparitions 41
Understanding Champion in Light of
Approved Marian Apparitions 49
Graces of Champion 111
What to Do When Visiting the Shrine 119

Part II

Prayers and Devotions

Preparation for Receiving the Sacraments. 131
Celebrating the Sacrament of Reconciliation . . 132
Celebrating the Eucharist 142

Celebrating the Anointing of the Sick 148
Praying the Rosary With Sister Adele 150
The Stations of the Cross 164
Novenas to the Queen of Heaven,
Our Lady of Champion 179
Additional Prayers and Litanies 226
Praying at the National Shrine 237

Appendix

The Original Devotion to
Notre Dame de Bon Secours 251
Timeline of the Historical Devotion to Our
Lady of Champion (N.D. Bon Secours) 260
Prayers to Our Lady of Champion 265
Hymns to Our Lady of Champion 274
Acknowledgments 280

A Note from the National Shrine of Our Lady of Champion

In 2023, the National Shrine received notification from the Holy See's Dicastery for Divine Worship and the Discipline of the Sacraments confirming the ability to celebrate an annual Solemnity Day on the grounds of the Shrine under the title of "Our Lady of Champion" every October 9 the established anniversary day of the Blessed Virgin Mary's second and third apparitions to Adele Brice in 1859.

Consistent with Champion Shrine's new Solemnity under the title "Our Lady of Champion," and in keeping with similar nomenclature used for other approved Marian Apparition Sites worldwide that take the name of the location where the apparitions occur, the Wisconsin Shrine will officially change its name to The National Shrine of Our Lady of Champion.

Not only did this step align more closely with other beloved Marian Apparition sites around the world, but it will also helped address any confusion that had existed in the past related to the Blessed Mother's title in reference to the National Shrine, titles such as Our Lady of Good Health, Our Lady of Good Hope, Our Lady Help of Christians, and Our Lady of Perpetual Help. In the message itself given to Adele Brice, Our Lady simply referred to herself as the "Queen of Heaven". The use of the name "Our Lady of Good Help" was reflective of the devotion that the Belgians had to Mary under that title for more than 200 years prior to their arrival in northeast Wisconsin. Champion in Belgium was also the location of the convent of Sisters who prepared Adele and her friends for their First Communion and Confirmation. Adele and her friends promised Our Lady at that time they would join the missionary work of the convent in Champion, a promise she could not keep when her parents emigrated to America. However, when the townspeople in the Wisconsin Belgian community, where Adele lived, petitioned and received permission from the U.S. Government for a new post office, the post office (and hence the town name) was changed to Champion. Thus, Adele did ultimately carry out a teaching mission with Our Lady . . . in Champion, WI!

Part I

Introductory Essays Concerning Marian Apparitions and the Shrine of Our Lady of Champion

Private Revelation, Biblical and Historical

The prayer book which you hold now is meant to aid pilgrims and devotees of an approved Marian apparition in the United States, commemorated at the National Shrine of Our Lady of Champion. The second section of the book contains many different devotionals, novenas, and prayers to help a person pray at the shrine and with the message Mary spoke. Before proceeding any further with the story of the apparition, its meaning, and significance in the life of the Church, it is necessary first to grasp the theology of private revelation, within which such manifestations fall.

Private revelation is not necessary for one's salvation because it is precisely that, private. If private revelation exists, that also means there must be public revelation. Public revelation refers to the revelation of Jesus Christ; it came to an end with the death of the last apostle. That means there can be no new public revelation. All private revelation must then relate to the public revelation of the Church.

The *Catechism of the Catholic Church* says this about public and private revelation:

> "The Christian economy, therefore, since it is the new and definitive Covenant, will never pass away; and no new public revelation is to be expected before the glorious manifestation of our Lord Jesus Christ." Yet even if Revelation is already complete, it has not been made completely explicit; it remains for Christian faith gradually to grasp its full significance over the course of the centuries.
>
> Throughout the ages, there have been so-called "private" revelations, some of which have been recognized by the authority of the Church. They do not belong, however, to the deposit of faith. It is not their role to improve or complete Christ's definitive Revelation, but to help live more fully by it in a certain period of history. Guided by the Magisterium of the Church, the *sensus fidelium* knows how to discern and welcome in these revelations whatever constitutes an authentic call of Christ or his saints to the Church.

> Christian faith cannot accept "revelations" that claim to surpass or correct the Revelation of which Christ is the fulfillment, as is the case in certain non-Christian religions and also in certain recent sects which base themselves on such "revelations."[1]

Benedict XVI offered the following commentary about private revelation:

> Consequently the Synod pointed to the need to "help the faithful to distinguish the word of God from private revelations" whose role "is not to 'complete' Christ's definitive revelation, but to help live more fully by it in a certain period of history". The value of private revelations is essentially different from that of the one public revelation: the latter demands faith; in it God himself speaks to us through human words and the mediation of the living community of the Church. The criterion for judging the truth of a private revelation is its orientation to Christ himself. If it leads us away from him, then it certainly does not come from the Holy Spirit, who guides us more deeply into the Gospel, and not away from

---

1 CCC 66–67.

> it. Private revelation is an aid to this faith, and it demonstrates its credibility precisely because it refers back to the one public revelation. Ecclesiastical approval of a private revelation essentially means that its message contains nothing contrary to faith and morals; it is licit to make it public and the faithful are authorized to give to it their prudent adhesion. A private revelation can introduce new emphases, give rise to new forms of piety, or deepen older ones. It can have a certain prophetic character (cf. *1 Th* 5:19-21) and can be a valuable aid for better understanding and living the Gospel at a certain time; consequently it should not be treated lightly. It is a help which is proffered, but its use is not obligatory. In any event, it must be a matter of nourishing faith, hope and love, which are for everyone the permanent path of salvation.[2]

Knowing the difference between public and private revelation, we might further ask, then why is there private revelation? Private revelation has biblical roots in its relationship to prophecy. The prophet Joel writes, "And it shall come to pass

---

2 Pope Benedict XVI, apostolic exhortation *Verbum Domini* (2010), no. 14.

afterward, that I will pour out my spirit on all flesh; your sons and your daughters shall prophesy, your old men shall dream dreams, and your young men shall see visions. . . . And I will give signs in the heavens and on the earth, blood and fire and columns of smoke" (Jl 2:28, 30). Paul also refers to prophecy in 1 Corinthians 12:10, Romans 12:6, and Ephesians 4:11. The visionaries of apparitions relate prophecy as they receive it through the received locations. Not only does the Bible provide a biblical foundation for apparitions, but the New Testament also provides an account of an apparition received by Jesus. When Jesus goes up Mount Tabor with Peter, James, and John, and the Transfiguration occurs, Jesus sees and talks with two Old Testament biblical figures, Moses and Elijah.

In the Catholic tradition, apparitions are not limited to those of Mary. Jesus himself has also appeared to individuals like St. Margaret Mary Alacoque (Sacred Heart devotion) and St. Faustina (Divine Mercy). Saints have appeared, and the Holy Souls in purgatory might visit and request prayers of individuals. The first reported Marian apparition was in Saragossa, Spain in the year AD 40 to St. James the Apostle. The devotion calls

Mary Our Lady of the Pillar, and the legends believes that Mary appeared to St. James (while she was still alive; that is, before her assumption) to encourage him in a moment when he despaired of his apostolic mission. Mary's apparition renewed his fervor to preach and gain converts for Christianity.

After a visionary receives an apparition, the Church enters into a process of discernment and investigation, and will later render a judgment regarding the veracity of the claim. The process of approving apparitions will be discussed later. Some of the more popular Marian apparitions include Guadalupe, Laus (apparition occurring between 1664 and 1718, receiving approval in 2008), Rue du Bac (Miraculous Medal), La Salette, Lourdes, Champion, Pontmain, Knock, Fatima, Beauraing, and Banneux. With all of these apparitions, their purpose was to renew the faith and foster a greater commitment to prayer and living the Christian life. And each of the apparitions and messages lends itself to deeper theological reflection and study. Every detail of the apparition is significant, from what Mary wears to what she says and even what she doesn't say. The location of the apparition also might convey a special meaning.

This prayer book will introduce you to the story, the message, and significance of an American apparition site in the state of Wisconsin. You will meet Adele Brise, the woman to whom the Queen of Heaven appeared relating a message of prayer and whom Our Lady "recruited" for service in the vineyard of the Lord. As is the case with all apparitions, the location has become a site of pilgrimage where people go seeking divine favor, petition the mother of God, and celebrate the sacraments. Your pilgrimage to Champion is only one leg of your greater pilgrimage from this life to the kingdom of heaven.

Mary Visits Wisconsin

For roughly 150 years, people in the greater Wisconsin area, the United States, and the world, probably did not even know that Mary appeared in Wisconsin. Or, if they thought so, it probably was to recall the condemned Marian apparitions claimed to have been received in the village of Necedah, Wisconsin. The names Our Lady of Good Help (Our Lady of Champion) and that of Adele Brise were foreign to most people, known only by locals within the Diocese of Green Bay. But today, in a rural setting, surrounded by farms in the country, a National Shrine pays tribute and offers pilgrims a place to pray at the place where the Queen of Heaven appeared to a twenty-eight-year-old immigrant named Adele Brise. This is her story. It is now more widely known, but it should be much better known still.

Marie Adele Joseph Brise was born in 1831 to Lambert and Catherine Brise in Brabant, Belgium. At a young age, an accident blinded her in one eye, but this did not affect her character; she was regarded as a pious young girl who loved God, the Blessed Mother, and everyone she met. At the time of her First Communion, Adele, along with a few other girls, promised the Blessed Mother that she would join a religious order of missionary sisters to teach children in foreign countries. By the 1850s, however, Adele's desire to join a religious order in Belgium seemed impossible, since her family intended to emigrate. Troubled, but relying on God, Adele sought the counsel of her parish priest who told her that she should obey her parents, and if God willed for her to be a sister, this would be realized in America.[3]

Lambert, Catherine, and their three children immigrated to the United States in 1855 and settled in the area of Red River, Wisconsin.[4] This area was populated with Belgian immigrants served by missionary priests, including Crosier Father Edward Daems and others who served in his absence.[5] In American Catholicism at that time, language

---

3 Sister M. Dominica, *The Chapel: Our Lady of Good Help* (De Pere, WI: Journal Publishing Company, 1955), 5.

4 Ibid., 5.

5 Ibid., 2–3.

barriers prevented many local Churches from serving pastoral needs. Ethnic churches were created to meet this challenge, but not in time to prevent the apathy of many immigrants regarding the practice of their faith.[6]

Adele lived a simple life with her family in the years leading up to her Mariophany on October 9, 1859. On the first occasion of the Blessed Mother's apparition, she was walking to the grist mill with a sack of wheat when she encountered "a lady all in white standing between two trees, one a maple, the other a hemlock."[7] Adele was frightened because she did not know who the visitor was. Eventually the vision disappeared, and she continued on her way. When relating the experience to her family, they believed her and presumed it to be a poor soul from purgatory in need of prayers. A few days later, Adele walked the same route on her way to Mass at the local church in Bay Settlement, eleven miles from her home. This time she was not alone but was accompanied by her sister Isabelle and a neighbor woman, Mrs. Vander Niessen. Adele again saw the lady. Much like the first time,

---

6 Ibid., 7.

7 Ibid.

the lady did not say a word, and the apparition quickly vanished, leaving Adele distraught. As she had done a few years earlier in Belgium when she needed advice, she went to confession following Mass and asked the priest for counsel regarding the two encounters. Fr. Verhoef, the parish priest in the settlement, advised Adele that if it were a heavenly messenger, she would see the lady again, and this time she should ask, "In God's name, who are you and what do you want of me?"

Upon Fr. Verhoef's suggestion that the visitor might return, Adele armed herself with the two questions. On the way home from Mass, again with her two friends, she encountered the same "beautiful woman, clothed in dazzling white, with a yellow sash around her waist. Her dress fell to her feet in graceful folds. She had a crown of stars around her head, and her long, wavy, golden hair fell loosely over her shoulders."[8] Kneeling, Adele opened her mouth, beginning a conversation with the Blessed Virgin Mary which would change her life forever:

> "In God's name, who are you and what do you want of me?" asked Adele, as she had been directed.

---

8 Ibid., 8.

"I am the Queen of Heaven, who prays for the conversion of sinners, and I wish you to do the same. You received Holy Communion this morning, and that is well. But you must do more. Make a general confession, and offer Communion for the conversion of sinners. If they do not convert and do penance, my Son will be obliged to punish them."

"Adele, who is it?" said one of the women. "O why can't we see her as you do?" said another weeping. "Kneel," said Adele, "the Lady says she is the Queen of Heaven."

Our Blessed Lady turned, looked kindly at them, and said, **"Blessed are they that believe without seeing. What are you doing here in idleness . . . while your companions are working in the vineyard of my Son?"**

"What more can I do, dear Lady?" said Adele, weeping.

"Gather the children in this wild country and teach them what they should know for salvation."

"But how shall I teach them who know so little myself?" replied Adele.

"Teach them," replied her radiant visitor, "their catechism, how to sign

themselves with the sign of the Cross, and how to approach the sacraments; that is what I wish you to do. Go and fear nothing. I will help you."[9]

The Queen of Heaven departed, lifting her hands as if beseeching a blessing. In a matter of minutes, Adele, a simple laywoman, uneducated but pious, received her vocation: to teach young people their catechism, how to make the sign of the cross, and how to receive the sacraments worthily. Her education was meager, and she knew it. She was a humble servant who did not regard herself as a fitting instrument of heaven, yet she was wise in the ways of the Lord. Anticipating her humility, the apparition provided precise instructions which were drawn from Adele's own instruction in the faith. She was not told to receive a loftier education, but to teach from her own love of God and the Blessed Mother. In doing so, she fulfilled the divine plan for her life.

Adele could not leave her experience along that Indian trail; it became a part of her being. Going forth from the apparition, having been sent as a missionary, Adele, mystified, returned home to

---

9 Ibid., 8–9.

share her encounter and message with her parents, sisters, and everyone she met. Immediately following the apparition, Adele devoted her life selflessly to the cause of catechesis. Her early method of evangelization spanned the course of seven years, traveling distances of fifty miles from home through all elements of weather. Walking from village to village, knocking on doors, she offered to do housework for families in exchange for permission to teach their children what the Queen of Heaven had prescribed.

Walking from home to home at great distances, one can easily imagine how exhausted Adele became. Impressed with her piety and willingness to follow her calling to these extremes, Fr. Phillip Crud, the newly appointed pastor to the Belgian colony, encouraged Adele to begin a life that others could share with her to fulfill the mission given to her by the Blessed Virgin. With a letter of solicitation and commendation from her pastor, Adele set out with a companion to begin the first of many begging missions throughout the settlement. Supported by others, Adele began a lay third order group of sisters, often called the Sisters of Good Health, but called the Sisters of St. Francis of Assisi by Adele.[10] Over the course of the years preceding her death, many young women joined the group of sisters for a short time. This tertiary group enjoyed recognition by the Diocese of Green Bay, and as such, they wore a religious habit and referred to each other as "Sister." In correspondences to Adele or about her work, the bishop often referred to her as *Soeur Adele*. Taking no formal vows, members were free to leave whenever they wished.

In the late 1860s, the Sisters of St. Francis of Assisi were instrumental in founding St. Mary's Academy, distinguished as the second school in the diocese. The sisters taught in both French and English, and Adele was responsible for the religious formation of the students. Often these students were orphans and other children who were sent there to have a better life. The school's foundation was a testimony to the trust in Divine Providence held by Adele and her companions. Accommodating more than a hundred children, the tuition was only a dollar a week. Adele wanted to make the education affordable and never turned anyone away for lack of funds. The dollar did not cover expenses, so the sisters begged for money, food, and other

10 Ibid., 16.

necessities. On one occasion, false rumors about Adele allowing the sale of alcohol at events reached the bishop. Accordingly, he demanded that Adele should send the students home and hand over the keys to the school. When Adele obediently arrived with the keys, she reminded the bishop that he would be responsible for the souls lost due to lack of instruction. Impressed by Adele's sincerity and her missionary zeal, he returned the keys and allowed the school to reopen.

On the eve of the twelfth anniversary of the apparition to Adele, a horrific event unfolded in Northeastern Wisconsin. During an extended drought, fire broke out in the small lumber village of Peshtigo.[11] Igniting on the same day as the Great Chicago Fire of much smaller proportion, the Peshtigo Fire was the most devastating fire in the history of the United States.[12] Fr. Peter Pernin, an eyewitness in Peshtigo on October 8, 1871, told how some survived that terrible day by taking ref-

---

11 Reverend Peter Pernin, *The Great Peshtigo Fire: An Eyewitness Account (Wisconsin)*, 2nd ed. (Madison: Wisconsin Historical Society, 1999), 16–18.

12 Martin W. Sandler, *Lost to Time: Unforgettable Stories That History Forgot* (New York, NY: Sterling, 2010), 181.

uge in the Peshtigo River and "involuntarily turning [their hearts] towards heaven as their only resource."[13] The fire tornado that began in Peshtigo then leapt across the bay and penetrated the Door Peninsula; its next visitation was Robinsonville, where Adele Brise, her sisters, and the wooden Chapel of Our Lady of Good Help stood in its determined path.

People in the Door Peninsula, particularly the area surrounding the Belgian settlement, were unaware of the happenings in Peshtigo. When the ferocious whirlwinds of explosive heat and flame overtook the territory, they believed that the end of the world was upon them.[14] The people of the area, staring death in its eye, took refuge at the Chapel of Our Lady of Good Help. Trusting in the intercession of Our Lady who had promised help to Adele, they begged for aid at the hour of their death. Adele was "determined not to abandon Mary's shrine . . . the children, the Sisters, and the farmers with their families, drove their livestock before them and raced in the direction of Mary's

---

13 Pernin, *The Great Peshtigo Fire*, 42.

14 Dominica, *The Chapel*, 19.

sanctuary."[15] The chapel had become filled with "terror stricken people beseeching the Mother of God to spare them, many wailing aloud in their fright. Filled with confidence, they entered the Chapel, reverently raised the statue of Mary, and kneeling, bore it in procession around their beloved sanctuary. When the wind and fire exposed them to suffocation, they turned in another direction and continued to hope and pray, saying the rosary."[16]

Praying for many hours outside of a Chapel, which by its very composition should have been incinerated by the torrential fire, and further the people should have suffocated from smoke inhalation, the people found relief in the early hours of October 9, the day commemorating the message given to Adele. Rain fell, quenching the fire.[17] Their prayers had been answered by the Lady of Good Help.

Fr. Peter Pernin, after hearing of the miraculous preservation of the Chapel of Our Lady of Good Help, journeyed to Robinsonville to see for

---

15 Ibid.

16 Ibid.

17 Ibid., 20.

himself. In the original manuscript entitled "The Finger of God," he recounts that "all the houses and fences in the neighborhood had been burned, with the exception of the school, the chapel, and fences surrounding the six acres of land consecrated to the Blessed Virgin. . . . [The property] sanctified by the visible presence of the Mother of God now shone out like an emerald island amid a sea of ashes."[18]

Twelve years previously, to the very day, Adele had been told that if people did not convert and do penance, Mary's Son would be obliged to punish them. At the time, people spoke about the Peshtigo Fire as fulfilling Our Lady's words to Adele about punishment. However, this cannot be stated with accuracy as there was no further revelation that confirmed this interpretation. Given this, one cannot ignore what resulted: a widespread, ready belief in the apparitions, sincere devotion to the Blessed Virgin, and a return to the faith and the sacraments. The Chapel of Our Lady of Good Help stood as a testament to the miraculous intervention

---

18 Peter Pernin, *The Finger of God*, an unpublished manuscript accessed through the Shrine of Our Lady of Good Help (Our Lady of Champion) archives.

of God through the intercession of his Holy Mother. Trusting in Mary's assurance of help and in her departing words to Adele, people believed that God could—and would—spare them through the intercession of the Blessed Virgin.

The physical threat to the chapel by fire soon became mirrored by a threat of spiritual dimension. Joseph Vilatte, a baptized Catholic, left the Church and was ordained a priest by the Episcopal Church for the Old Catholic Church. He moved to the Belgian territory and began seeking to gain converts to his sect. The Old Catholic Church was formed in the late 1800s because they did not accept papal infallibility. As such, the Old Catholic Church denied the Immaculate Conception, confession, and indulgences; they also viewed clerical celibacy as optional and celebrated Mass in the vernacular.[19]

During his tenure in Wisconsin, Vilatte took residence in the town of Duvall at St. Mary's Old Catholic Church, where he erected an Old Catholic church between two Catholic churches.[20] Due to the number of people flocking to his sect, Adele

19 Dominica, *The Chapel*, 24.

20 Ibid.

became concerned with the loss of souls and so faithfully prayed that he would do no more harm and convert. Bishop Messmer became aware of the growing heresy in the Peninsula and invited Fr. Pennings and the Canons Regular of Premontre, also commonly referred to as the Norbertines, from Berne Abbey in Holland to the diocese to combat this heresy. In 1895, Pennings began an annual pilgrimage to the chapel "to beseech Mary's help against the evil work and influence of Vilatte" and to catechize the people of the settlement.[21] The Old Catholic Church was unable to flourish in the Door Peninsula, because Catholics who might have been drawn to the sect were unwilling to accept implementation of their reforms, especially public confession and the abolition of Mary's cult.[22] Vilatte's failure to gain converts to Old Catholicism in Wisconsin led him elsewhere, but by the end of his life, he confessed his wrongdoing and remorse for having supposedly seduced 500,000 Catholics and sought a return to the Catholic Church. After recanting his heretical beliefs, he took up a life of

21 Ibid., 25.

22 Ibid., 26.

penance at the Cistercian Abbey of Pon-Colbert, Versailles, where he died as a layman.[23]

Vilatte's bid to evangelize and convert people to Old Catholicism had been preempted by the Blessed Mother. Her triumph over heresy was marked in the end by faithful people who could not forego their Marian piety. Vilatte's conversion marked another milestone in the life of Adele Brise. As in 1871, when the faithful had gathered with her in prayer at the Chapel to spare their land, Adele's prayers were answered for the conversion of Joseph Vilatte and the demise of the heretical sect. Adele Brise died on July 5,1896, with her last words being, "I rejoiced in what was said to me. We shall go into the house of the Lord."

On a Sunday morning of October 1859, Adele Brise experienced a heavenly vision of the Blessed Virgin. Very few in the history of the Church have received this privilege. For the thirty-seven years following that apparition, Adele's life was marked by a specific call to evangelize. Her life, witness, zeal, and mission testify to her love of the Lord and the Blessed Mother. Adele Brise and the Chapel of

---

23 Msgr. Joseph Marx, "Vilatte and the Catholic Church," *The Salesianum* 37, no. 3 (July 1942): 113–20.

Our Lady of Good Help share a rich history, not only with the Diocese of Green Bay, but with the United States and the Americas. Her insignificant role in history is intensified because it shares in the continuity of the Marian dimension of evangelization, specifically in the New World to the present day. The message of Champion, Wisconsin is becoming more widespread and has an ever greater urgency in this millennium. How the message will play out in the history of the American Church in this new age, the age of the New Evangelization and missionary discipleship, remains to be seen.

Analyzing the Apparition

Years before the Wisconsin apparition received ecclesiastical approval, I was speaking to a priest friend of mine who belonged to a religious congregation. I shared with him the story of Mary's apparition and specifically her message. After I finished telling him the story, he commented that it seemed the apparition had more of a personal nature to it. He suggested that apparitions like Lourdes or Fatima had a universal appeal. Although received by one seer or a couple visionaries, once the message was conveyed to the world, it was meant to be lived by all people. He perceived Mary's message to Adele to pray for the conversion of sinners, celebrate the sacraments, and teach the children as a personal mission, and one carried out by Adele, a completed task. While certainly, he may be right that there was a personal dimension to the apparition and message, nevertheless, the mission given to Adele didn't end with her death but was handed on to others and is passed on to us today. There is a universal dimension to the apparition as it invites us to join our prayers to Mary's for the conversion of the world, to celebrate the sacraments and intentionally offer our Holy Communion for the conversion of sinners, and then to live the mission of sharing the faith with others in some capacity.

In 2010, when I began my initial study of the Champion apparition and presented my study at the Mariological Society of America, I employed a method of analyzing the apparition proposed by Fr. James McCurry, OFM Conv, who in his 1992 presidential address to the society, analyzed the Guadalupan apparition in light of Mary's name, message, and mission. When analyzing the mission given to Adele, I specifically proposed a two-fold approach, the first being the contemplative nature of the apparition—that is, the call to prayer—and secondly, an active component, which was the teaching of the faith. Nine years now removed from my initial study, I still hold true to my original thesis, but further reflection has helped me to understand the Champion apparition especially in light of Mary's role as a catechist, more specifically the lessons she taught at Champion.

The Lessons Mary Taught at Champion

The Rosary has often been called the school of Our Lady in which we quietly contemplate with Mary and learn from her the different aspects of Jesus's life. Meditating on Our Lady might also lead us to consider her role as an educator of Jesus. Did she teach Jesus his prayers? How to read? In the pages of Sacred Scripture, Mary teaches the reader by her example. We learn from her surrender to God's will, humility, obedience, and generosity, among other virtues. When Mary appeared in Champion to Adele Brise, the message she spoke contained many lessons. As we study Our Lady and the Wisconsin apparition, we become a student in her "school" and learn from her heavenly lesson plan. These are Mary's lessons.

Lesson One: Mary Teaches Us About Herself and Her Heavenly Mission

The opening words of Mary's dialogue with Adele were this: "I am the Queen of Heaven who prays for the conversion of sinners." As Catholics we hail Mary under the title of Queen in different ways. She is the Queen of Mercy, Queen of Angels, Queen of

Apostles, and Queen of Peace. One can learn the many regal titles of Our Lady from the Litany of Loreto. In this apparition, Mary reveals her exalted heavenly dignity meditated upon in the fifth glorious mystery of the Rosary and written about by Pius XII in his encyclical *Ad Caeli Reginam.*

In telling Adele that she is the Queen of Heaven, Mary reveals the fullness of her eschatological identity and conveys a sound biblical theology. Theologians like Dr. Edward Sri and Dr. Scott Hahn have written extensively on the *gebirah*, or Queen Mother theology. We can rightly call Mary queen because this was the custom found in the Old Testament (see 1 Kgs 2:19; 2 Kgs 9:27; 11:3; 24:15; Jer 29:2; 2 Chr 22:12). The queen was not the wife of the king, but rather his mother. Jesus, as King of the Universe, shares his royalty with his mother Mary, who is the Queen Mother. What was the role of the Queen Mother? To serve as the intermediary, the advocate, and intercessor for the common people. When individuals had a concern, they would bring it to the queen who would voice it to her son the king. Mary continues to fulfil this role as the intercessor of humankind. Marian shrines testify to this reality that the people approach Mary, ask her prayers, and she intercedes and advocates for them before the throne of her divine Son. Mary affirms the Queen Mother theology by telling Adele what she does in heaven, specifically praying for the conversion of sinners. She advocates, she pleads before her Son for the conversion of the world. This is what any loving queen would do for her people. This is what Mary has done. And perhaps, this is the very reason why she appears to the chosen visionaries: out of love for the world.

Lesson Two: Mary Invites Us to Participate in Her Mission

Not only does Mary tell us who she is and what she does, but she also invites us to participate in her heavenly mission. She told Adele, "I wish you to do the same." When it comes to Marian devotion, we often ask Mary's intercession. We do this all the time in the Hail Mary, asking Mary to pray for us now and at the hour of our death. Our Lady teaches us that there is more to Marian devotion than just seeking intercession. We are encouraged to imitate our Lady. We are asked to pray with her and to join our prayers to hers. When we pray for the conversion of sinners, we join the prayer of Mary before the throne of Jesus.

Lesson Three: Mary Promotes the Sacraments

In all of Mary's apparitions, she does not direct the focus to herself. Instead, Mary wishes to draw the attention to her Son. Mary wants people to know Jesus and to worship him. In the Champion apparition, Mary reveals a lesson about the sacraments, the necessity of confession, and the reception of Holy Communion for the conversion of sinners. Mary teaches us that we must seek God's forgiveness for the sins we have committed, and further, she teaches a lesson in Eucharistic theology.

Mary specifically told Adele to offer her Holy Communion for the conversion of sinners. This is an exercise of the baptismal priesthood of all believers being called to offer sacrifice and prayers to God. At every Mass, the priest invites the faithful to "pray brothers and sisters that my sacrifice and yours might be acceptable to God the almighty Father." In the offering of the Holy Sacrifice of the Mass, we join our prayers and petitions to that of the priest and of the Church. Mary's lesson to Adele was to offer her Holy Communion for the conversion of sinners. The moments following our reception of the Eucharist are powerful and, according to the dictates of Our Lady, a moment in which we can pray for the conversion of sinners. The apparitions at Fatima taught a similar Eucharistic theology and the same is true for the apparitions of Jesus received by St. Faustina.

Lesson Four: Mary Prepares Us Spiritually for Mission

One of the neglected aspects of the Champion apparition is the spiritual dimension of the message and mission. Much emphasis is given to the latter part of the apparition, the commissioning of Adele to teach the children what they need to know for salvation. Because of the perceived lack of catechesis during that period of American Church history, many believe the catechetical component to be the most important aspect of the message. One must not forget the spiritual component of prayer and celebration of the sacraments.

The lesson Mary teaches Adele is the need to spiritually prepare for mission. If Adele was going to labor for the conversion of sinners, she had to first be converted herself by acknowledging and confessing her sins through a general confession. She then was to pray for the conversion of sinners by offering her Holy Communion for that intention; in so doing, Adele would be praying for those whom she would teach, those who were away from the regular practice of faith. It is from the sacramental life of the Church and our personal prayer that we draw strength for the mission that God has entrusted to us.

Lesson Five: Mary Gives a Warning

Mary offers a startling statement, "If they do not convert and do penance, my Son will be obliged to punish them." Some people find it hard to accept this statement, and because of this aspect of Mary's message, some wish to dismiss the apparition because it does not correlate with their theology of a loving, forgiving, and merciful God. First, we must acknowledge that Mary's statement is a conditional. If they do not convert and do penance, my Son will be obliged to punish them. This is a warning. The reality remained that we can change. We could prevent destruction and punishment.

Some people look at this statement as one of chastisement. It could be. There was no further revelation to confirm this, so one must discern from the events that occurred whether or not this was what Our Lady meant. Another approach to understanding this statement might be to realize the consequence of sin. Sometimes sin itself brings about consequences. If I lie, the truth might be discovered, and as a result, I will suffer. If a person contracepts and then wishes to conceive, there might be sterility or infertility.

Mary's lesson invites us to a conversion of life. But conversion alone is not enough. Our Lady asks us to do penance or, in other words, to make reparation for our sins. Have we listened to Our Lady's message? Do we strive to convert our lives? Have we done penance?

Lesson Six: Mary Commends Faith

When those with Adele could not see Our Lady, they asked Adele why they couldn't see the woman. Mary responded, "Blessed are they who believe without seeing." This is a direct quote from the Scripture, which tells us that Mary knows the words of her Son. Each time we profess our faith, every time we visit the shrine and seek Mary's intercession, we can hear Our Lady say those words about us, "blessed are they who believe." As pilgrims to the shrine, we accept the testimony of Adele Brise that Mary appeared to her. When doubt creeps into your life, hear those words of Our Lady, let her affirm your faith and belief.

Lesson Seven: Don't Be Idle

Mary asks Adele a question: what are you doing here in idleness while your companions are working in the vineyard of my Son? For Adele, this was a reminder of her promise to become a missionary and work in the foreign missions. Our Lady wishes to rouse us into action. The stories of the saints and others who dedicate their lives to God can inspire us to action. If you believe God has been calling you to do something, don't delay any longer, instead choose to act.

Lesson Eight: Mary Wants Conversion Through Action

If one word could summarize Mary's message to Adele, it would be conversion. After all, that is how Mary identifies her heavenly mission, and she asks Adele to pray for the conversion of sinners. The active component of Mary's message—namely, to gather the children and teach them the faith—could be seen as an extension of the mission of conversion. When a person comes to know Jesus Christ, and the Gospel message, he is invited to convert their lives and conform them to the teaching of Jesus. Our Lady teaches us that praying for conversion is not enough; we must do more. A teaching component can complement our prayers and facilitate the answer to our prayers. We might ask ourselves if there is an area of our lives that needs greater conformity to the Gospel message? If there is, we can and must pray for the grace of conversion; it may be appropriate or even necessary for us to take an active role in the conversion of our minds and hearts. For example, if we struggle with the Church's teaching on contraception, we should pray for a conversion of our intellect and heart, and perhaps read literature to understand the Church's position. Consulting Paul VI's *Humanae Vitae* or a talk from Dr. Janet Smith might help us better understand the Church's teaching. If we struggle with the issue of premarital sex, then we could read the Church's teaching as expressed through the Theology of the Body. If we desire conversion in our lives, it means we might have to take an active role in facilitating it.

Lesson Nine: Mary Gives Us a Method of Evangelization

The message of Our Lady and the active mission entrusted to Adele was to teach the children. As the Belgian immigrants made their way to the United States and settled in Wisconsin, many were falling away from the practice of faith because they were not being accompanied by pastors. A language barrier between the immigrants and clergyman in the area existed. This prompted Fr. John Perodin to pen a letter to the Church in Belgium asking for priests to join them in America.

Our Lady's message proposes what could be called the Champion Formula of Evangelization. Parents coming to the United States with their children stopped practicing their faith. Consequently, their children did not know the saving mysteries. Thinking about the current state of the Church in post-modernity, one might notice a similar situation. Parents not practicing their faith and children going to catechism class but not engaging the faith on a regular basis or "making it their own." As Adele traveled throughout the Door Peninsula to spread the Gospel, she entered the homes of families and instructed the children. Her outreach to the littlest of the families perhaps had greater reach also to the parents. This is precisely what I mean by the Champion Formula of Evangelization. In the third millennium, parents still feel obligated to send their children to religious education classes, even if they do not regularly practice the faith themselves. The Church today must provide an encounter with the person of Jesus Christ, the Church, and the sacraments. Once the heart of the child, teenager, or young adult is touched by Christ's transforming power, families will begin to experience conversion themselves. A young person's engagement with the faith might cause curiosity on the part of the parents and lead them into an encounter with Christ and the Church. Mary gives a formula of evangelization that worked for Adele during her life and, by chance, might still be applicable in the Church today.

Lesson Ten: Mary Gives a Lesson Plan

Our Lady told Adele quite specifically what it was she should teach the children: their catechism, how to approach the sacraments, how to make the sign of the cross, and what they need to know for salvation. To summarize, the lesson plan is all of Christianity. Thus, applying the message of Our Lady today would entail teaching the official Catechism of the Catholic Church and its four parts as we have received it: the creed, Christian mystery, life in Christ, and Christian prayer. The lesson plan of Our Lady given to Adele should invite Catholic parishes, religious education programs, and Catholic schools to first seek the salvation of souls. Everything we do must be about the salvation of souls. If not, then it doesn't seem to align with this heavenly lesson plan of catechesis.

Lesson Eleven: Mary Promises Help

Mary's parting words to Adele were: "Go and fear nothing, I will help you." Adele truly experienced Mary's help throughout her missionary life. Mary's help comes in the assurance of prayers and the mediation of grace. Mary's help extended to Adele in her missionary sojourn throughout the wild country, with the foundation of a tertiary order of sisters and a school, preservation from the Peshtigo Fire, and the putting down of a spreading heresy. Today, Mary's promise of help is offered to the pilgrim who prays at the shrine in a time of need. While on our exile here below, we rely on the prayers of Mary and her help so that one day we might become citizens in the kingdom of heaven.

Conclusion

Our Lady came as a catechist, teaching heavenly lessons to Adele Brise, whom she invited to serve as a missionary catechist in Northeast Wisconsin. The mission that Adele received did not end with her, but she entrusted it to others. As pilgrims, the story of Adele touches our hearts and invites us to participation in the same mission of prayer, sacramental celebration, and catechesis. The response of each person will be different. Our Lady's invitation and the Lord's call for each of us are unique to who we are. But now, and always, they demand our response. How will you live Our Lady's mission? Let Mary teach you, not only the lessons that she taught in Champion, but also how to love God and neighbor, how to pray, and how to get to heaven. Sit for a while as a student in the school of Our Lady, and then live the lessons you learn every day.

Method of Approval for Marian Apparitions

On December 8, 2010, Bishop David Ricken in a historic decree, for the first time in United States history, legitimized a Marian apparition. The approval came 151 years after the apparitions were received by Adele Brise in 1859. The process of approval for other prominent Marian apparitions occurred quicker than the Wisconsin decree. In the cases of some of the more prominent apparitions, the need necessitated a quick examination and statement by the Church. In the case of Lourdes, France, a spring of water healed people miraculously. In Fatima, the sun spun in the sky and was witnessed by tens of thousands. There was a pressing need for the Church to investigate and make a statement regarding the apparitions.

In the case of Champion, the need was not as apparent. Some might contend that the Peshtigo Fire might have been a good reason to examine the claims of Adele, but officially no investigation took place. People readily believed Adele's claims of apparitions, perhaps in part due to her more mature age when contrasted to the children who saw the Blessed Virgin in Lourdes or Fatima. Events like the Peshtigo Fire only confirmed what people already believed, that Mary appeared to Adele.

While no official inquiry into the apparitions was made until Bishop Ricken launched a commission to investigate the historicity and theology of the apparitions, the Church seemed to grant an implicit approval in various ways. Bishops allowed for the celebration of the sacraments, they visited the property, and even celebrated the Mass themselves, customarily on August 15. In 1977, the US apostolic nuncio, a Belgian, Archbishop Jean Jadot celebrated a special liturgy at the shrine on August 5 and 6 of that year. Suffice to say, the presence of the local ordinary granted credence to devotion and belief in the apparitions.

Nonetheless, it is important for the Church to make statements regarding the veracity of such claims. That is why in 1978 the Congregation for the Doctrine of the Faith released a decree on the "Norms regarding the manner of proceedings in the discernment of presumed apparitions and revelations"[24] The twentieth century saw a proliferation of people claiming private revelations. The Church decided to delegate the discernment of private revelations to the local ordinary, and this document established both positive and negative criterion to look at. The positive criteria include the establishment of fact that the apparition occurred, the character of the visionary, theological inerrancy in the message, and the devotion of the people. Negative criteria could include errors of fact concerning the apparition, theological error, profit or gain from the apparition, immoral acts of the visionary or followers, and the manifestation of psychological issues with the visionary. After a period of inquiry, the bishop can make a statement regarding the supernatural nature or lack thereof. An apparition could be determined to be *constat de supernaturalitate, non constat de supernaturalitate*, or *constat de non supernaturalitate.*

---

24 An online version may be accessed at: http://www.vatican.va/roman_curia/congregations/cfaith/documents/rc_con_cfaith_doc_19780225_norme-apparizioni_en.html

In the case of the Champion apparition, Bishop Ricken convened a commission of three scholars who examined the history of the Wisconsin apparition, evidence of claims, and the long history of the shrine. After a period of discernment, Bishop Ricken believed it possible to claim with moral certainty that supernatural events did occur in the life of Adele, with the apparitions and locutions (messages) she received.

In a 2012 German article,[25] theologian Emery de Gaàl cited eight further criterion of evaluating Marian apparitions proposed by Marian theologian, and one of the greatest experts on Marian apparitions, René Laurentin. They include:

1. Whether there is a concordance with Church teaching (gospels, faith, and moral doctrine)
2. Whether the seer is selfless, truthful, and spiritual, or even saintly

---

[25] Emery de Gaal, "Zu einer Kriteriologie fur Mariophanien-Die Marienerscheinungen in Robinsonville/Champion im Bistum Green Bay (Wisconsin, USA)." *Sedes Sapientiae: Mariologisches Jahrbuch* 16, no. 2 (2012), 35-59. I received an English translation of the article.

3. Whether the external signs—such as spiritual or physical healings—correspond with the message
4. Whether there are recognizable spiritual fruits (orientation towards Christ)
5. Whether the person and message are congruent
6. Whether the recipient is capable of disseminating the message with success
7. Whether a supernatural quality can be attributed to the apparition
8. Whether the message is edifying[26]

The following cursory review yields a favorable outcome when examining Champion.

1. The message is congruous with the Scriptures and gospel. Elements of the message include Old Testament theology related to the Queen Mother. The message of conversion resonates with Jesus's call to repentance and the sermon on the mount. Mary quotes Sacred Scripture

---

[26] Emery DeGaal, quoting Rene Laurentin, "Marienerscheinungen" in Wolfgang Beinert and Heinrich Petri (eds.), *Handbuch der Marienkunde* (Regensburg: Pustet, 1984), 528-555.

when she commends Adele's companions for their faith in what is unseen. Finally, the evangelical component of the message reminds us of Jesus's exhortation to the disciples to make disciples of all nations. In effect, by teaching the gospel, Adele did just that in her local community.

2. Adele was known for devoutness. She had a desire to be a religious sister before immigrating to the United States, and the last apparitions occurred on her way to and from Holy Mass.
3. Healings occurred immediately during the life of Adele and people continue to claim healings today. The preservation of the shrine property from the Peshtigo Fire and the defeat of the Vilatte heresy are examples of spiritual fruit.
4. The spiritual fruits of the apparition to this day include prayer and celebration of the sacraments, especially Reconciliation and the Eucharist.
5. Adele strove to live the message she received and dedicated her entire life to executing it.
6. Adele readily shared the apparition with those she met in different capacities. She shared snippets of the experience in letters she wrote

to families, with those she met on begging missions, and also with appropriate ecclesiastical authorities (her pastor in the first days, and then with the appropriate hierarchical figures).

7. After an investigation done more than 150 years later, the local bishop decreed the likelihood of supernatural quality.
8. The message continues to build up the faith and inspires people to this day.

As a final note, while the Church approves Marian apparitions as worthy of belief, the Catholic faithful are not obliged to believe in them. What a Catholic must assent to is public revelation, that is the gospel and tradition taught by Christ and the apostles. Marian apparitions comprise private revelation and do not require our belief. For those devoted to the sites of Mary's many apparitions, they find the messages to be uplifting and helpful to living their Christian faith. Hopefully that is what you find with the Champion apparition: encouragement to pray often for the conversion of sinners and an invitation to teach and share your faith with others.

Some Unapproved Apparitions to Know

In the United States alone there are several unapproved Marian apparitions, meaning the local bishop examined the apparition, the life of the seer, and the theology of the message and determined it to be at odds with the Catholic faith. In the state of Wisconsin, the alleged apparitions in Necedah fall within this category. Other unapproved apparitions include Bayside, New York, Scottsdale, Arizona, Conyers, Georgia, and Covenant of Love in Toledo, Ohio.

Instead of following condemned apparitions, I recommend staying close to the messages of approved apparitions like: Guadalupe, Rue du Bac, Lourdes, Champion, Fatima, Knock, Beauraing, and Banneux.

Understanding Champion in Light of Approved Marian Apparitions

Mary has appeared in many locations throughout history, but only a few of those apparitions have ever been validated or approved by the Church. Champion joins an elite group of apparitions including Guadalupe, Lourdes, and Fatima, among others. Why does Mary appear? She appears at particular moments in history to guide God's people back to him. In her apparitions, she never brings the focus on herself, but always directs us to the sacraments—to the Eucharist and Penance. In Guadalupe, Lourdes, Fatima, and Beauraing, Mary desired that a church be built—a place where Mass would be offered and people could come and pray. Mary desires to put a wayward people back in a right relationship with their heavenly Father. As a loving mother, Mary comes to guide us on our way toward salvation.

In reading about any Mariophany, one will notice many similarities, especially Mary's desire for the salvation of souls. The conversion of sinners seems to be a typical theme for most messages. In reading the story of Juan Diego, one can find many similarities between Adele Brise and Juan Diego regarding their lives, message, and mission received. In this chapter, Champion will be analyzed in light of other approved apparitions. To a certain degree, all Mariophanies are related, and one can notice a progression in the message, as if a torch has been passed on to Mary's next revelation. Mary's message and mission to Juan Diego is a similarly lived message and mission in Champion by Adele. The apparitions of Champion and Lourdes could be viewed as bookends to each other. Fatima could be viewed as an intensification of the Champion message and mission. Lastly, Our Lady's apparition to a Belgian immigrant in 1859 is mirrored by another Mariophany to five Belgian children in Beauraing, Belgium. These apparitions should not be seen in isolation from one another but in complete complementarity. Private Marian revelation should be viewed as a collective whole. When we situate the Wisconsin apparition within the context of other approved Marian apparitions, we can better understand the significance of Our Lady's message to Adele.

The Parallels of Guadalupe and Champion

The year was 1519; Spanish conquistadors led by Hernando Cortes just arrived in the New World to explore and colonize New Spain.[27] Upon landing, they discovered the Aztec civilization, the mode of governance of the colonies and the religion of the Aztec people—the worship of the gods and goddesses: sun, rain, wind, and fire.[28] Their worship extended to the point of offering sacrifices to appease the gods or to prevent future misfortune.

---

27 The Handbook of Guadalupe provides two chapters on the Evangelization of the New World; see: Bro. Francis Mary, FFI, "Catholic Spain in the Evangelization of the New World" in *A Handbook on Guadalupe* (New Bedford: Academy of the Immaculate, 1997), 19-23. And: Diana Cary, "Cortes and the Valiant "Little Ladies" in *A Handbook on Guadalupe*, 35-40.

28 Francis Johnston, *The Wonders of Guadalupe* (Rockford: TAN Books and Publishers, 1981), 12.

Unlike the biblical notion of offering animals in sacrifice, "they felt driven to supply this divinity [the sun] with a regular 'nourishment' of human blood," typically the blood of slaves or prisoners of war.[29] Christian missionaries arrived in an attempt to Christianize the colonies, but for the most part, they were unsuccessful. A spiritual crisis was emerging.

Over three hundred years later in the United States of America, a wave of immigrants from Europe arrived.[30] Local churches became overwhelmed with the pastoral need to address the growing immigrant church throughout the country causing the rise of national churches.[31] Like the

---

29 Johnston, 12-13.

30 Marcus Hansen provides a brief commentary on the language problems for immigrants in his work *The Immigrant in American History*. See: Marcus Hansen, *The Immigrant in American History* (Cambridge: Harvard University Press, 1942), 146-7. Another work addressing the issue of immigration is: John F. Kennedy, *A Nation of Immigrants* (New York: Harper and Row, 1964), 17-63.

31 Jay Dolan provides a good commentary on the rise of national churches. C.f. Jay Dolan, *In Search of An American Catholicism* (New York: Oxford University Press, 2002), 60-61; 133-134.

rest of the United States, Northeastern Wisconsin saw its share of immigrants especially those of Belgian descent. As the Belgians settled in the Door Peninsula, in 1853, missionary Crosier Father Edward Daems provided for their sacramental care; however, after his transfer by the diocese to another post, it would be three years until his return.[32] In the interim, Rev. John Perrodin made infrequent visits to the peninsula, and in a letter to a European pastor, he wrote, "For the spiritual account unfortunately there is much to lose for the Catholic emigrant. . . . They end up by neglecting their duties of religion and live as unbelievers. The children are not instructed and grow up without knowing God. . . . Would there be any priests in Belgium zealous enough to accompany their flocks?"[33]

Suffice to say, the faith of the Belgians suffered because they were without a spiritual father who would instruct them on a regular basis. A spiritual crisis was emerging.

Besides the evident spiritual crises both in Mexico in the 1500s and Northeastern Wisconsin in the 1850s, these two events share more in

---

32 Dominica, 1-2.

33 Ibid., 3.

common. In time and space, both were places of intervention through a Mariophany to two visionaries—Juan Diego and Adele Brise. There are many similarities between Guadalupe and Champion, beginning with the implied message of evangelization and extending to the life and mission the visionaries undertook as a result of the apparition. This chapter will show the interconnectedness of the two apparitions in light of the visionaries' lives and visions and the content of their respective Mariophanies.

The Early Lives of Juan Diego and Adele Brise

The more contemporary apparitions of the Blessed Virgin Mary, of which arguably the most popular are Lourdes and Fatima, share a similarity—the visionaries or seers were young children or adolescents born into poor peasant or lower-class families. In Guadalupe, something entirely different is found. While it is true Juan Diego was poor and merely educated to the extent of preparation for the workforce,[34] Our Lady appeared to some-

---

34 Dr. Charles Wahlig, "Juan Diego: Ambassador of Heaven" in *A Handbook on Guadalupe* (New Bedford: Academy of the Immaculate, 1997), 44.

one who was not a child, but was "already in the prime of life."[35] Similarly, Adele, who came from a poor immigrant working family and received a very meager education in Belgium,[36] received her apparition at the age of twenty-eight. Prior to their respective Mariophanies, both were considered to be devout, pious persons.[37] The Blessed Virgin chose Juan Diego and Adele to receive a message along with a specific mission. Mary did not choose children for the task of catechesis or to relay her message to the world; instead, she chose poor and unlearned instruments who would be capable of transmitting the faith through teaching others by the witness of their lives.

Wahlig provides a commentary on the contemporary discussion pertaining to Juan Diego's poverty. The class to which Juan Diego belonged was a property-owning class either from inheritance, working, or both. The poverty of Juan Diego in historical study concludes he undertook it voluntarily.

35 Fr. Christopher Rengers, O.F.M. Cap, "Mother of the Americas" in *A Handbook on Guadalupe*, 3.

36 Dominica, 5.

37 For the testimony regarding Adele's virtue see Dominica, 6. For testimony regarding Juan Diego see Johnston, 24-5; Wahlig, 44.

The Message

Juan Diego and Adele's apparitions came at a particular junction in their lives in which their vocational calling was made clearer vis-à-vis the content of the message and the mission they received. The days in which both saw the Blessed Virgin and received their message were marked by the same occurrence—they were on the way to and/or[38] from Mass. Juan Diego and Adele both had to walk long distances from their homes to arrive at the church; for Juan Diego, it was a nine-mile journey,[39] and Adele had to make an eleven-mile trek.[40] The key phrases contained within Juan's dialogue with the Virgin in relation to the Champion apparition are as follows:[41]

---

38 The second and third apparitions received by Adele occurred on Sunday October 9, 1859, first on the way to the church and then upon her return from Mass. It was during the third apparition Our Lady spoke to Adele. During the first apparition, Our Lady did not relay a message then either.

39 Wahlig, 46; Johnston, 25.

40 Dominica, 8.

41 The content of the dialogue with Juan Diego is taken from the Nican Mopohua as found in A Handbook on Guadalupe, 193-204.

In the first apparition:

1. Our Lady asked Juan where he was going.
2. Mary identifies herself as the ever Virgin Holy Mary, Mother of the God of truth.
3. Juan Diego was told that he would be the means by which Mary's compassionate and merciful objective would be achieved.
4. Mary acknowledged her gratitude and promised to help him as she sent him forth on his mission.

Second apparition:

5. Juan Diego begged Our Lady to send one of the nobles who were held in high esteem and respected to convey her message to the bishop.

The dialogue between Juan Diego and Our Lady was similar to that between Adele and the Queen of Heaven. In her identification at Tepeyac as the Holy Virgin Mary, Mother of the God of truth, Mary places her identity as Mother of the true God in contrast to the Aztec gods whom the Indians were worshipping. Even though Juan Diego had already been converted, Mary's name would be important in relaying her identity in his work of evangelization. Mary places herself in a distinct way from the Aztec goddess Tonantzin[42] and appears over the site of where a temple once stood to this pagan goddess.[43] As the Mother of the true God, Mary replaces Tonantzin and beckons the Indians to the true God—Jesus Christ. In Champion, Mary identified herself as "the Queen of Heaven who prays for the conversion of sinners."[44] It would appear the connection that both identifications shared was Our Lady's desire for the salvation of souls. She desired the conversion of the Aztecs, and she desired the return of the Belgians who had become lax in the practice of their Catholic faith. In both ways, Mary reveals the *sitz im leben*[45] (oppressed Aztec culture—alienated, impoverished French Belgian Door County)—the need for conversion to the Catholic faith.

Our Lady asked Juan Diego where he was going. He was headed to the church for Mass and instruction on the feast of the Immaculate Conception (then observed on December 9). For Adele,

---

42 Johnston, 13.

43 Ibid.

44 Dominica, 8.

45 German theological term in biblical criticism meaning "setting in life."

she had seen Mary on her way to Mass and spoke with her on the way back. The Queen of Heaven commended Adele for her reception of Holy Communion but exhorted her to do more—to pray for the conversion of sinners through the offering of future Holy Communions and to make a general confession.

The importance of Adele's preparation for her mission also reflects the fact that Juan Diego could only fulfill Mary's wishes by going to the bishop and requesting that a sanctuary be built in her honor. In the same way, Adele was the instrument through which Our Lady's objective of catechesis and conversion would be brought about. Juan Diego and Adele both felt unqualified for the mission. Juan Diego requested that Mary send another noble person to speak to the bishop, while Adele asked Our Lady, "But how shall I teach them who know so little myself?"[46] Adele did not believe herself to be worthy of the mission because she was a poor, uneducated immigrant who was blind in one eye. Nevertheless, Our Lady found her to be qualified because she could teach from her own knowledge of faith and from her relationship with the Lord.

46 Dominica, 9.

Furthermore, the Mariophany she received would become the conduit of teaching as she relayed the marvelous event to those she met.

Lastly, both were sent off with a blessing and promised help from Mary. Juan Diego was told that even in "the fatigue, the work and trouble that my mission will cause you" he would be rewarded.[47] Juan Diego would face the rejection of the bishop after his first visit and suffer other afflictions, but in the end he would be rewarded as proven with the *tilma* and the widespread belief that followed. Adele was told, "Go and fear nothing, I will help you."[48] Like Juan Diego, Adele suffered adversity, rejection by some in the community, the loss of Belgians to the Old Catholic heresy,[49] and temporary ecclesiastical problems because of misunderstandings that reached the bishop.[50] But through

---

47 Handbook, 196

48 Dominica, 9.

49 In the Door Peninsula, Joseph Rene Vilatte, an Old Catholic priest, sought to gain converts to his heretical sect. C.f. Dominica, 24-26.

50 At times in the life of Sr. Adele's ministry, false rumors had spread to the bishop which caused him to place a temporary interdict on the chapel and closing the school. After conversing with Adele, admiring her zeal

it all, Adele received the heavenly guidance and intercession of Mary. Even amidst their lowliness and unworthiness to undertake their missions on behalf of heaven, Juan Diego and Adele went forward from their apparitions sent as missionaries to those they encountered—spreading the gospel of Jesus Christ and the story of their private encounter with Mary.

Mission

The Franciscan Renewal Center in Scottsdale, Arizona, features an outdoor shrine and altar to Our Lady of Guadalupe. In addition to a large image of *La Virgen*, a mural of Juan Diego gathering people and sharing the story of the apparition as he displays the *tilma* can be found. The image depicts Juan Diego as a missionary who traveled the surrounding area to share the story of the apparition and gain converts. The message of Guadalupe, accompanied by Juan Diego's mission, resulted in the massive conversion of the native people. Conversion accounts are numerous with claims of nine

---

for the salvation of souls, he ordered the school and chapel to be reopened. Cf. Dominica, 21-22.

million conversions, stories of priests performing six thousand baptisms per day, and an account of how one priest baptized over one million people throughout his life.[51]

Juan Diego was a layman and a convert. At one time he was married, but his wife died prior to Mary's appearance.[52] Following the reception of Mary's message and the *tilma*, Juan Diego was placed "in charge of the new chapel, to which a room was added for his accommodation . . . [where he] devote[d] the rest of his life to the custody of the new shrine and to propagating the story and explaining the significance of the apparitions."[53] Helen Behrens commented that "he told [the Indians] the story of the apparitions and repeated the loving words of the Blessed Virgin over and over again, thousands of times, until all knew the story. When the Indians presented themselves to the missionaries, they had already been converted by Juan Diego."[54]

---

51 Johnston, 56-7.

52 Carl Anderson, *Our Lady of Guadalupe: Mother of the Civilization of Love* (New York: Doubleday, 2009), 5.

53 Johnston, 54-5.

54 Helen Behrens, quoted in Johnston, 55.

Juan Diego's mission was to inform the bishop of Mary's desire for a church to be built at the site of the apparition so that she could be the Mother of the Afflicted. However, his mission extended beyond that simple and specific mission. It entailed an even broader mission to share the message he had received so that others may acknowledge Jesus Christ as the true God. Through Our Lady and her apparition, the faith was entrusted to millions through her simple messenger, Juan Diego, first to the bishop but then to the rest of the New World.

When viewing the image of Juan Diego teaching with the *tilma*, one cannot help but see the parallel between Juan Diego sharing the story of the *tilma* and Adele's mission of teaching the young people their catechism, how to make the Sign of the Cross, and how to approach the sacraments. Similarly, Adele could be pictured in the fields of the Door Peninsula or on the chapel property with children gathered around her, intently listening to her story of Mary's marvelous apparition. Adele's missionary zeal led her on a mission going from house to house and offering, unsolicited, to do whatever work there was to be done in the household—asking only in return that she be permitted to give instruction to the children. Rain, snow, or heat did not prevent her from accomplishing her work; neither did fatigue or ridicule have any effect upon her.[55]

Seven years after these missionary efforts in a fifty-mile radius, Adele settled near the chapel built by her father and upon the instruction of Fr. Phillip Crud, who "advised her to encourage others to share her labors. . . . He urged her to appeal for funds, to build a Convent and school where the children could come to her for instruction."[56] By 1867 and 1868 the convent and school had been established, and Adele's lay tertiary group, the Sisters of Good Help (often referred to erroneously as the Sisters of Good Health), "was established, and recognized by the Bishop of the diocese as a regular auxiliary of the Church."[57] Fr. Crud's vision was realized, and Adele began a more centralized and localized means of catechesis for the young people in accord with her mission. While Adele did not convert a nation or millions, she worked diligently for the salvation of souls, one by one, in her missionary efforts.

---

55 Dominica, 9-10.

56 Ibid., 11.

57 Ibid., 14.

Juan Diego and Adele were both lay people whom the Blessed Mother had entrusted with a specific mission. While Adele is often referred to as "Sister" Adele, the order of sisters she found were a lay tertiary group of Franciscans. In the 1850s, it would have been common to refer to tertiaries as "Sister," and there are records of Adele being called *Soeur* by the bishop[58] and others who knew her. Timothy Matovina cites the hagiography of *Huei tlmanhuicolitca* which "depicts Juan Diego as a model Franciscan lay brother."[59] If this is the case, vocationally, both visionaries lived the life of

---

58 In a letter dated December 10, 1895 obtained from the Diocesan archives, Bishop Joseph Fox writes, "There is a place, however -- Robinsonville with Soeur Adele -- where they could put the boy and the board would be very cheap." The letter was in response to a request for a boy to be accepted into an orphanage run by the diocese.

59 Timothy Matovina, "Theologies of Guadalupe: From the Spanish Colonial Era to Pope John Paul II" Theological Studies 70, 2009, 70. C.f. Anderson, 132. Anderson's treatment of Our Lady of Guadalupe includes a chapter on Juan Diego's vocation in which he provides a synopsis of the situation regarding the barring of Indians from Holy Orders. In 1539 the bishops permitted Indians to join minor orders.

lay Franciscan brother- and sisterhood. They lived their vocations through catechesis and as custodians of the respective chapels built to foster devotion to Mary. Secondly, in carrying out their mission, Juan Diego and Adele became the vehicles through which Mary's messages were conveyed. Juan Diego had a distinct instrument for catechesis, the *tilma*, while Adele had clear instructions what to teach the young children. Thirdly, both were involved in the sacramental preparation for those whom they catechized. Juan Diego presented to the missionaries the converts he had gained for baptism, while Adele presented the children to the local priest for examination and admittance to Holy Communion.[60] Fourthly, both worked in cooperation with their bishop; even when Adele found herself at odds with the local bishop, she obediently followed his directives. Lastly, Juan Diego and Adele faithfully lived their missions. Juan Diego sought out the bishop to have a church built, at which he served for the rest of his life. Adele faithfully taught the local children by walking around the settlement but also through the establishment of a

60 Dominica, 10.

school and a convent. Both died having lived a life worthy of the call and mission they had received.

Conclusion

Guadalupe and Champion share a number of parallels in their visionaries' respective lives and missions. Notably, both apparitions occurred in the Americas, making them American[61] apparitions, and both had a purpose within their given timeframe. Our Lady came at a pivotal point in the evangelization of the New World in 1531 and ushered in the conversion of millions. The missionaries' program was not working, so Our Lady came with her tool for evangelization; namely, the *tilma*. Similarly, in 1859, when immigrants were falling away from the faith and not preparing their children for the sacraments, Our Lady instructed Adele to teach young people the basics of the Catholic faith.

Since the promulgation of Paul VI's encyclical *Evangelii Nuntiandi*, coupled with the pontificates of John Paul II and Benedict XVI, a term has

61 This term is used loosely in this context to refer to North, South and Central America.

become popular: "the new evangelization", which refers to ways in which to make the gospel relevant in today's world. In the fall of 2012, a synod of bishops was convened in Rome to address the new evangelization. In the United States, the USCCB Committee on Evangelization and Catechesis released a document entitled "Disciples Called to Witness," reflecting on methods of evangelization in America. Further, the pontificate of Pope Francis has emphasized missionary discipleship. The Church can look to Juan Diego and Adele, who were missionary disciples called to witness in their respective times in history in order to facilitate the conversions. Their witness still inspires the Church today as it comes to a better understanding of catechesis. With the recent approval given to the Champion apparition, evangelization has begun to take a more visible place within the Catholic Church in America. With pilgrims visiting each day, praying at the site of the apparition, receiving Holy Communion and absolution, asking Mary to "pray for us sinners," and visiting Adele's grave, they too are being taught by Adele.

The legacies of Juan Diego and Adele continue to this very day, and their messages should be seen not in opposition but in tandem with each other. Their historical settings, lives, messages, and missions can assist the Church today in understanding how to respond to the current crisis of faith—a crisis of atheism and relativism. In a time when a new evangelization is needed and has been called for, these Marian apparitions can become guiding principles, allowing Mary to become the guiding star. May our own halting efforts at sharing the Christian message with others be guided by the Star of the New Evangelization, the Virgin Mother of the true God and the Queen of Heaven. May the Church, through her intercession and by the inspiration of St. Juan Diego and Sister Adele, gain converts to the Catholic faith as did Mary's faithful messengers so many years ago.

Lourdes and Champion: Bookend Apparitions

One of the most popular apparitions of the Blessed Virgin Mary occurred in 1858 in the small village of Lourdes. Today, the sanctuary of Our Lady of Lourdes attracts millions of pilgrims each year. They come to pray at the Grotto of Massabielle, to bathe in the waters, and to make processions in accord with the requests of Our Lady.

The seer was a young girl named Bernadette Soubirous. She suffered health problems early on in her life and her family was quite poor. On February 11, 1858, Bernadette accompanied her siblings to collect firewood at the local dump. It was there that Bernadette began to converse with the lady who would later identify herself as the Immaculate Conception. Our Lady appeared a total of eighteen times, with the final apparition occurring on July 16, 1858. During the series of apparitions, Mary requested prayers especially for sinners and asked Bernadette to do penance for the sins of the world.

How are we to understand the connection and interplay between these two apparitions which occurred on different continents? The first consideration is that of timing. The apparitions occurred within just a little more than a year of each other (February 11, 1858-Lourdes, October 9, 1859-Champion). In one sense, it could be said that the apparitions bookend each other. This is true especially because of Mary's revealed name. To Bernadette, the woman identified herself as the Immaculate Conception. To Adele, the beautiful lady said she was the Queen of Heaven. In Lourdes, Mary speaks about the beginning of her life; that is, her conception and the recently defined dogma of 1854. In Champion, Mary emphasizes the fullness of her exalted identity in heaven. After completing the course of her life on earth, having been assumed body and soul into heaven, she now reigns as Queen of Heaven and Earth. The identity of Mary given to these two seers demarks the beginning and the end of Mary's life.

There are similarities between the visionaries too. Even though Bernadette was a teenager and Adele a woman in her late twenties, what they share is their sickness (Bernadette, asthma, Adele, eyesight) and meager education. Both received their apparitions while in the wilderness, undertaking tasks for their family. And after the apparitions, both dedicated themselves to religious vocations. The requests Mary made to the women were also similar. Pray for sinners and do penance. One difference relates to the request for a church to be built. Mary does not request a church in Champion but does so in Lourdes. Even with that, Adele's message emphasized the sacraments of Reconciliation and Eucharist, both of which are celebrated within the confines of a church.

There also was a catechetical component to both apparitions. At the time of Our Lady's apparitions in Lourdes, Bernadette had not yet made her first Holy Communion. This has led some Marian scholars to suggest that Mary prepared Bernadette for her First Communion. In the apparition received by Adele, she was instructed to teach the children how to receive the sacraments. Once her task was complete, Adele presented the students to the priest, who then administered to them their first Holy Communion. In one, Mary is the teacher; in the other, Mary commissions a teacher of the faith.

Our Lady also asked that the pilgrims make processions when they visit Lourdes. To this day, an evening rosary procession occurs during pilgrimage season. While not a request in Champion, processions do occur. One might say the first procession was on the night of the Peshtigo Fire when the local townspeople processed with the statue of the Blessed Virgin. This procession is re-lived each October 8. On the feast of the Assumption each year, a Eucharistic Marian procession also takes place with all the gathered faithful.

When Our Lady appears, she often chooses the most humble and unqualified to receive the message. The messages she relays are often similar and complementary. Certainly these two qualities are much in evidence when we consider the respective apparitions received by Bernadette and Adele.

Fatima and Champion: Eucharistic Reparation and the Conversion of Sinners

In 1917, in the village of Fatima, Portugal, Mary, under the title of Our Lady of the Rosary, appeared to three shepherd children—Lucia dos Santos and her cousins Jacinta and Francisco Marto. Prior to Mary's appearance to them, the children received three apparitions of an angel, who called himself the Angel of Peace. Between the angelic apparitions and those of Our Lady, a common theme emerges from the Fatima apparitions: prayer for the conversion of sinners, Eucharistic reparation, the Rosary, and prayer for world peace. Given the message these children received, Fatima can be seen as an intensification of the Champion message. It is a further development of Mary's message and mission to Adele, in which we find a change in the language Our Lady used.

The Angelic Apparitions: Adoration and Reparation

In 1916 and 1917 the three shepherd children were taught specific prayers of adoration and reparation by the Angel of Peace. During the first angelic apparition, the children were taught the following prayer: "My God, I believe, I adore, I hope and I love you. I ask pardon of you for those who do not believe, do not adore, do not hope and do not love you."[62] No prayer was taught during the second angelic apparition, but the angel encouraged them to pray and offer sacrifices "as an act of reparation for the sins by which [God] is offended and in supplication for the conversion of sinners. You will thus draw down peace upon your country."[63] In the third and final angelic apparition, the angel had in his possession a communion host and chalice for adoration, and he taught the children the follow-

62 The quotations and descriptions about the Fatima apparition come from Lucia's memoirs as quoted in: Mark Miravalle, "Marian Private Revelation: Nature, Evaluation, Message, in *Mariology: A Guide for Priests, Deacons, Seminarians and Consecrated Persons* (Goleta, CA: Queenship Publishing, 2007), 863.

63 Miravalle, 864.

ing prayer: "Most Holy Trinity, Father, Son, and Holy Spirit, I adore you profoundly, and I offer you the most precious Body, Blood, Soul and Divinity of Jesus Christ, present in all the tabernacles of the world, in reparation for the outrages, sacrileges, and indifference with which he himself is offended. And, through the infinite merits of His most Sacred Heart, and the Immaculate Heart of Mary, I beg of you the conversion of poor sinners."[64]

Following the prayer, the angel then distributed the Eucharistic species to the children—the Host to Lucia and the Precious Blood to Jacinta and Francisco. Upon reception of Holy Communion, the angel said, "Take and drink the Body and Blood of Jesus Christ, horribly outraged by ungrateful men! Make reparation for their crimes and console your God."[65] These three angelic apparitions' message was reparation for sin made through the personal offering of the Eucharist.

Fifty-seven years earlier in Champion, the same themes were present. At the core of the Champion apparition was the conversion of sinners through prayer and catechesis. Adele was instructed to

---

[64] Ibid., 865.

[65] Ibid.

offer her Holy Communion for the conversion of sinners. The instruction to the Fatima children to do likewise was intensified by the request to also make an offering of reparation. It was necessary for the children to console God and to ask pardon for those who do not believe, adore, or love him. Secondly, the angel's requests were unique because they allowed for the children to exercise the common priesthood of all believers received in the sacrament of Baptism by offering the reception of the Eucharist for those specific intentions. For Adele and the Fatima children, begging the Lord for the conversion of sinners through prayer, sacrifice, and offering Holy Communion became their lifelong ministry.

The Apparitions of Our Lady

Mary appeared in Fatima on the thirteenth of each month (with the exception of August, when the visionaries saw Our Lady on the nineteenth because they were imprisoned on the thirteenth), beginning in May and culminating in October, when the great miracle of the sun occurred.[66] In the first

---

[66] Ibid., 874.

apparition, Our Lady asked the children if they would be willing to accept suffering in reparation for sin as an act of supplication for conversions. She also asked them to pray the Rosary every day for world peace. In all, she basically reiterated the angel's requests for sacrifice and reparation. In the second apparition, on June 13, Mary said that Jesus desired to establish a devotion to her Immaculate Heart in which salvation would be promised to the devotee. During July's apparition, she instructed the children to make sacrifices and taught them a prayer: "Sacrifice yourselves for sinners, and say many times, especially whenever you make some sacrifice: 'O Jesus, it is for love of you, for the conversion of sinners, and in reparation for the sins committed against the Immaculate Heart of Mary.'"[67]

The Blessed Mother also showed the children a vision of hell and told them the current war was going to end. However, if people did not stop offending God, a worse war would break out. To this end, Our Lady stated that she would "ask for the conversion of Russia to [her] Immaculate Heart, and the Communion of Reparation on the First

---

[67] Ibid., 871.

Saturdays."[68] Lastly, she taught what has come to be known as the Fatima Prayer, said after the Glory Be when reciting the Rosary: "O my Jesus, forgive us our sins, save us from the fires of hell. Lead all souls to heaven, especially those who are most in need of thy mercy." In the fourth apparition on August 19, Mary simply reiterated the children's mission to prayer, as, according to her, many souls go to hell because no one prays or sacrifices for them. The fifth apparition emphasized the need to pray the Rosary for world peace. In the sixth and final apparition, Our Lady revealed her name as the Lady of the Rosary. She added that people "must amend their lives and ask forgiveness for their sins."[69] Then St. Joseph appeared with the child Jesus, and Mary appeared as Our Lady of Dolors and Our Lady of Mount Carmel. Following the apparition, the sun began to spin and cast multicolored light. Over seventy thousand people witnessed this miracle.

---

68 Ibid., 872.

69 Ibid., 876.

The Five First Saturdays

Following the Fatima apparitions, Francisco and Jacinta soon became victims of the influenza epidemic and died soon thereafter as Our Lady had revealed to them. Lucia entered the Sisters of Saint Dorothy and later entered a cloistered order of Carmelite sisters in Coimbra.[70] It was during her time as a Sister of St. Dorothy, on December 10, 1925, that Our Lady, with the Child Jesus, appeared to Lucia a seventh time. The devotion of the Five First Saturdays, which Mary had previously recommended during the third apparition, was further explained to Lucia. Lucia beheld the pierced and wounded Hearts of Jesus and Mary, which are pierced by blasphemies and ingratitude. Lucia was encouraged to make reparation through the First Saturday devotion. Those who "confess, receive Holy Communion, recite five decades of the Rosary and keep [Mary] company for fifteen minutes while meditating on the fifteen mysteries of the Rosary, with the intention of making reparation to [the Blessed Mother]" would be assisted at the hour of death and given the graces necessary for

---

70 Joseph A Pelletier, A.A., *Fatima: Hope of the World* (Worchester, MA: Washington Press, 1954), 131.

salvation.[71] Our Lady was thus relaying a specific formula in which reparation could be made. Just as Adele was told, in preparation for her mission, to make a general confession and offer her Communion for the conversion of sinners, Our Lady was preparing Lucia and countless others who have observed this tradition over the years. Mary was revealing her desire for the salvation of souls by calling souls to return to the sacraments, to prayer and contemplation. By going to the source of all strength, individuals would experience a conversion of their lives through the sacraments, and perhaps the fidelity of those Catholics who make reparation may encourage someone else to conversion and to make similar reparation. In both Champion and Fatima, Our Lady revealed a spirituality centered on the sacraments, specifically the Eucharist and Penance, which would result in personal conversion along with the intention of converting others.

---

71 Miravalle, 878.

Amendment of Life

In both Champion and Fatima, Our Lady asked that sinners do penance and amend their life. This is evident from her wish that visionaries pray for the conversion of sinners and, in the case of Fatima, make reparation. In Champion, it is even more evident than Our Lady's conditional statement: "If they do not convert and do penance, my Son will be obliged to punish them." In Fatima Our Lady said, "If people do not cease offending God, a worse [war] will break out during the pontificate of Pius XI. When you see a night illumined by an unknown light, know that this is the great sign given you by God, that he is about to punish the world for its crimes, by means of war, famine, and persecutions of the Church and the Holy Father."[72]

Mary came to warn the people that they must convert from their sinful ways. As seen in the language shift from Champion, which emphasized the sole need for prayer for the conversion of sinners, to Fatima's pressing need to make reparation, it seems that the world had entered into a moral decline in which a celestial intervention—that is, an

[72] Ibid., 872.

appearance of Mary—was necessary. All throughout the Fatima apparitions, Mary encouraged the children to pray the Rosary for peace in the world. If the world did not want to see war, famine, and persecutions, people would have to turn away from sin, do penance, amend their lives, and pray, especially the Rosary. If Mary's requests were heeded, war would be prevented. As with Champion, the so-called chastisement language does not necessarily need to be seen as a punishment inflicted upon the human race but rather as a natural result of man's lack of conversion. Famine results because of man's greed and selfishness, and persecutions of the Church arise out of man's personal ideologies. The remedy for these "punishments" due to sin is amendment of life and prayer, which Our Lady requested at both Champion and Fatima.

Conclusion

At Fatima, Our Lady reiterated the message she had previously given to Adele. In this light, Fatima can be seen as a continuation of Champion in which Mary asks for personal conversion and a mission of prayer, reparation, and sacrifice for the conversion of sinners. The lives of Jacinta and Francisco were a testimony to suffering because they willingly took on suffering for the sake of conversions.[73] Lucia faithfully carried out her apostolate of prayer as a religious sister and most especially as a Carmelite nun later in life. Adele and the Fatima children remained faithful to what Our Lady had requested of them. The relevance of both apparitions is omnipresent in our society today, as evidenced by the continual moral decline and assault on the Catholic Church, to say nothing of the moral rot within the Church.[74] Throughout the centuries, Mary has intervened at specific moments in history and spoken a message calling humankind to repentance. We must willingly respond to Our Lady's apostolate of prayer for the conversion of the world, which she requested at Champion and Fatima through the offering of Holy Communion. If we are faithful to Mary's request, perhaps what she had promised us at Fatima—world peace and the conversion of the world—will be obtained.

---

73 Francis Johnston, *Fatima: The Great Sign* (Washington, NJ: AMI Press, 1980), 101.

74 In the United States this is best exemplified by the assault on religious liberty which may force the closure of Catholic hospitals, universities, etc.

Belgian Immigrants and Belgian Children: Beauraing, Banneux, and Champion

Beginning on November 29, 1932 through January 3, 1933, five Belgian children, Fernande, Gilberte, and Albert Voisin; and Andrée and Gilberte Degeimbre, received a total of thirty-three apparitions of the Blessed Mother. Mary relayed exceptionally simple messages to each child, encouraging them to be good and to pray often. Throughout the apparitions, Mary revealed to them her Golden Heart. In her final apparitions at Beauraing, Our Lady identified herself to one of the children as the Mother of God, the Queen of Heaven.

Since the apparitions of Beauraing, researchers and scholars have written about how the apparition served as a continuation or a fulfillment of previous Marian apparitions. Don Sharkey and Joseph Debergh, OMI, proposed that Beauraing is a sequel to Fatima.[75] H. M. Gillett relays the account of the bishop of Tarbes and Lourdes who "publicly declared last summer in the pulpit at Lourdes: 'The cultus of Our Lady of Beauraing completes magnificently that of Lourdes. . . . Lourdes and Beauraing

---

75 Joseph Debergh, O.M.I., *Our Lady of Beauraing* (Garden City, NY: Hanover House, 1958), 145.

are the complements of one another."[76] As others have argued in the past for the complementarity of Beauraing and other such Mariophanies, the same can be said of Beauraing and Champion, perhaps even to a greater degree, given that the visionaries shared the same nationality and that Mary identified herself with the same name to Andrée as she did to Adele. Many similarities then are found between the two—the setting and description of Mary, the life situation, the message, the names, and the fact that each apparition served as a place of prayer at particular moments in history.

The Apparition: Setting and Description of Mary

Even though great distances separate the two locales, Champion and Beauraing share a common setting for each apparition, as they each occurred between or under one or more trees. In Champion, all three apparitions occurred at the same location—between a maple and a hemlock tree. During the sixth Beauraing apparition on December 1, 1932, Our Lady appeared "below the arched

---

[76] H. M. Gillett, *Famous Shrines of Our Lady vol 1* (The Newman Press: Westminster, Maryland, 1952), 252.

branch of the hawthorn tree."[77] For Beauraing, the setting is appropriate, as the city's name means "beautiful branch."[78] The same cannot be said for Champion. The maple and hemlock trees between which Mary appeared have no significance to the name of Champion. Spiritually, however, one could suggest the two trees represent the Tree of Life and the Tree of the Knowledge of Good and Evil.[79] Since Mary encouraged prayer for the conversion of sinners and catechesis of young people, individuals would be presented with two choices: whether to live only from the Tree of Life or to eat the bad fruit of the Tree of the Knowledge of Good and Evil. The choice was theirs whether to accept Our Lady's request and be nourished by the Tree of Life or to ignore it and fall prey to the Tree of the Knowledge of Good and Evil. The hawthorn tree and the maple and hemlock trees are significant because it was Mary who chose to appear in these symbolic locations.

The pilgrims who come to the Shrine of Our Lady of Champion after hearing the description

---

77 Debergh, 46.

78 Ibid.

79 C.f. Genesis 2:9 (RSV)

of what Mary looked like during her appearance question whether or not she would appear with long, golden, wavy hair. Their reaction is normal given the stereotypes associated with Jewish women. Jewish women are stereotypically characterized with darker hair and dark eyes. Mary's appearances to Adele and the Beauraing children are at odds with the stereotypical image of the Blessed Virgin as a traditional Jewish woman. In Beauraing, Gilberte said Our Lady had blue eyes.[80] While these two minute details, the color of Mary's hair and eyes, seem insignificant, they are extraordinarily revealing. In other apparitions—for example, Our Lady of Guadalupe and Our Lady of Kibeho—Our Lady appeared in ways that would be familiar to the visionary or visionaries. Appearing in native Aztec dress, Our Lady and her message to Juan Diego became more appealing because the native people were more apt to accept her message as one of them. Would golden hair (characterized for our purposes as blonde) and blue eyes have been a familiar way for Our Lady to appear to the Belgian people? There is at least some acknowledgment of Belgians having blonde hair, as one of the parents,

---

[80] Debergh, 149.

Marie Louise Perpete, is described as having blonde hair.[81] The way in which Mary appeared to Adele and the Beauraing visionaries suggests, at the very least, that in both apparitions Mary appeared in a way in which she would not look foreign. She instead appeared as one of them. She revealed herself to be a loving mother who wished to dialogue with her children, and in order to make the message acceptable, she appeared in a way familiar to the respective visionaries.

Lastly, there are similarities in Mary's attire. Adele described Mary as a "beautiful lady, clothed in dazzling white, with a yellow sash around her waist. Her dress fell to her feet in graceful folds. She had a crown of stars around her head . . . such a heavenly light shone around her that Adele could hardly look at her sweet face."[82]

The Beauraing children described Mary in a similar fashion but with some notable differences. In describing Our Lady's appearance, Gilberte answered, "She wears a white dress shot with blue—as if it were reflecting something blue. The hem of her dress hides her feet and mingles with the white

---

81 Ibid., 43.

82 Dominica, 8.

cloud on which she stands. Her hands are clasped together. . . . She smiles and she has a white veil on her head which falls over her shoulders and comes nearly to her knees. There are rays of light all around her head, very straight and narrow."[83]

The rays of light Gilberte described "formed a dazzling diadem for [Mary's] head."[84] Given the descriptions of Mary at Champion and Beauraing, Mary similarly wore a white dress, had rays of light surrounding her head, and wore a diadem or crown. At Champion, the white dress fell gracefully to Mary's feet, and in Beauraing, the hem of her dress hid her feet. This white dress could be the symbol of Mary's purity. The crown which Mary wore symbolizes the name she revealed to the visionaries—the Queen of Heaven. As with the trees and Mary's blonde hair and blue eyes, these are simply factoids, yet they suggest similarities shared between the apparitions and set the scene for even greater similarities between Champion and Beauraing.

---

83 John Beevers, *The Golden Heart: The Story of Beauraing* (Chicago: Henry Regnery Company, 1956), 25.

84 Ibid., 17.

The purpose in showing the similarities is noteworthy, given that the apparitions were received by individuals of Belgian heritage. While Beauraing may be the completion of Lourdes and the sequel to Fatima, it shares much in common with Adele's apparition. Regardless of the apparitions' locations, Mary's appearance, and her apparel, these details emphasize continuity between Mary in her communication with the Belgian people; namely, Adele and the five Beauraing children.

The Life Situation

At Champion and Beauraing, a general theme or reason for Mary's need to intervene at those specific moments in history can be identified: spiritual apathy. The Belgian people's (in America) spiritual crisis due to the lack of a pastor has been referenced several times in this book.[85] As a result, the Belgian immigrants to Northeastern Wisconsin fell away from the Church. The same was true for the Walloon population in Belgium, who "without being atheists, were far from being fervent

---

85 For further cross reference, see: Dominica, 3.

Catholics."[86] In fact, Gilberte's family had not practiced their faith for a number of years, and her father, Hector, was known to frequently attend Socialist Party meetings.[87] Given the apparent spiritual crisis that was plaguing Belgium and even more specifically the Voisin family, the choice of Mary's place of appearance seemed appropriate to bring about a spiritual renewal within Belgium and the Voisin household. From the beginning, Mrs. Voisin wavered in her belief but mostly accepted the children's claims. She even encouraged them to pray and consult the parish priest, Fr. Leon Lambert. Later she even asked the priest to celebrate a Mass in honor of Mary so that a sign might be given that the apparitions were true.[88] Mary's appearance to the Beauraing children brought about a renewal of their families' faith, and as time would tell, throughout all of Belgium, as thousands would gather and pray at the apparition site.

While it is uncertain if the Brise family was practicing their faith (with the exception of Adele and her sister, Isabelle) or if they themselves had

---

86 Debergh, 43.

87 Ibid.

88 Ibid., 47, 48-49.

become prey to the spiritual crisis of the Northeastern Wisconsin Belgian settlement, what we do know is that Lambert and Catherine Brise accepted Adele's claims of visions. After the apparitions, her parents helped her in every way to ensure the message their daughter had received would be spread throughout the area. To Adele and the Beauraing children, Mary's apparitions occurred at a time people's faith needed renewal, and it would be precisely through these apparitions in Champion and Beauraing that the people's faith would be renewed and the faithful would have a new spiritual home in which they could make pilgrimages and request the Blessed Virgin's intercession. Of course, the purpose of Mary's apparition was not to glorify herself but to provide motherly guidance for her children so that they might experience the fullness of their faith in Christ Jesus. Her apparition brought the faithful back to the sacraments, reconciling them with the Church and providing lasting implications for their ultimate eternal destiny. It was out of love for the world that Mary appeared to Adele and the Beauraing children at a time of spiritual crisis.

The Message

The apparitions of Beauraing are unique in that Mary spoke to each individual child, either asking them a question or making an extremely simple statement. As at the Champion apparition, it could be said that Mary spoke in personal and general terms. When she asked Fernande, "Do you love my Son? Do you love me?" Our Lady was asking her a personal question, but it was a question which could be asked of all who heard the story of the apparition. Thus, like the analysis of the Champion apparition in name, message, and mission, it could be said that Our Lady relayed a personal message and universal mission; namely, to pray always. Beauraing's mission was simple because the visionaries themselves were simple; they were children. They were not yet at a state in life to work as Adele did, so their mission was simply to be good and pray always. This simple message nevertheless parallels that which Adele received.

On December 2, Our Lady instructed the children to "always be good."[89] She also asked them,

---

89 Ibid., 223. Subsequent quotations containing the dialogue Mary had with the Beauraing children should be assumed to have come from Appendix A of Debergh, p. 223-24.

"Is it true that you will always be good?" Mary was asking the children to amend their lives—to no longer lie or talk back to their parents, but to live the commandments. However, this personal question encourages all people to consider the ways in which they offend God. A simple request to always be good means so much more. For Adele, it meant to go to Mass and receive the sacrament of Penance so as to turn away from sin in order to assist others in living the Christian life. To the children whom Adele catechized, she was telling them to always be good, as she showed them how to make the Sign of the Cross and taught them the faith. At Champion more than seventy years earlier, Our Lady essentially gave the same instructions to Adele that she would later give to the Beauraing children—always be good. This simple phrase can thus be seen as a continuation or a reminder to the Belgian children to live a life worthy of the gospel message.

It cannot be emphasized enough: Mary's message to the Beauraing children was striking in its simplicity: "Pray. Pray very much" and "Pray always." As a result, they were being called to a contemplative mission—to pray for the world and for one another. The children's mission of prayer was meant not only for them but also their families, the parish, and the greater community—the world at large. It is a simple reminder for the world to enter into silence and to commune with God. Again, we can view the message and mission of Beauraing as a simplification of the message and mission of Champion, and rightly so, since Our Lady was dialoguing with children. Adele's mission of prayer for the conversion of sinners was not to be a one-time affair; rather, it was something that she continuously kept before her since it was combined with her apostolic mission of catechizing. Adele was to pray always for the conversion of sinners because, as she was reminded, if they do not convert and do penance, the Lord would be obliged to punish them. This warning was an impetus to Adele's fidelity in her prayer life and apostolic zeal. The mission of prayer was central to both Champion and Beauraing.

During the final apparition in Beauraing on January 3, 1933, Our Lady again asked a series of poignant questions to Fernande: "Do you love my Son? Do you love me?" Of course, Fernande said yes to each question. How could she not love Jesus and Mary, having been privileged to encounter heaven on earth? Our Lady's response to Fernande's answer was, "Then sacrifice yourself for me." Fernande was receiving a specific duty to sacrifice herself for Jesus and Mary. Mary did not specify the type of sacrifice required, so it could have meant self-sacrifice, or perhaps dedicating more time to prayer, or maybe even exerting herself to do more service to the Church and the community. The idea of sacrificing oneself could also be found in Adele's life and ministry. Our Lady asked Adele, "What are you doing here in idleness while your companions are working in the vineyard of my Son?" Following this question, Our Lady requested Adele to sacrifice herself by gathering the children and teaching them the Catholic faith. For Adele, her sacrifice was to give her life away in order that the young and old alike would be able to hear the gospel message and have the means to amend their life. The questions Our Lady posed to Fernande and Adele could similarly be asked of us. We are called to think about what more we can do for the Lord. Do I pray enough? Do I own too much? Do I support the Church financially and through my own service? If not, then sacrifice yourself for Jesus, Mary, and the Church. Sacrifice your time, your treasure, and give of your talent. Maybe your idleness can be remedied as Adele's was by instructing young people or through service at a local food pantry. You need only turn to Matthew 25, the Corporal Works of Mercy, or Catholic Social Teaching to find ways in which you can sacrifice yourself for the good of the Church and others.

During the apparitions in Champion and Beauraing, Our Lady spoke similar messages. Most interestingly, in the thirty-three apparitions of Our Lady at Beauraing, she did not always speak, she only revealed herself to the children. She abided with them and prayed with them. She revealed her Golden Heart. Similarly, at Champion, Our Lady appeared three times, speaking only in the third apparition. Our Lady manifested herself quietly to Adele in order to prepare her. In both apparitions, the visionaries were called to deeper communion with Jesus and Mary through prayer and were told to amend their lives in different ways. The apparitions to the Beauraing children in 1932 and 1933 mirror those Adele received in 1859. To the Belgians, Our Lady was giving a reminder that God exists and that they must live lives worthy of the kingdom, which meant to pray and to always be good. To this day, the message and mission entrusted to these visionaries continues through those who read or hear about the apparitions or make pilgrimages to those holy sites.

The Names of Mary

In the Mariophanies throughout history Mary has often revealed a specific name to the visionaries. A few examples include Lourdes (Immaculate Conception), Fatima (Lady of the Holy Rosary), and Kibeho, Africa (Mother of the Word). Apropos Beauraing, Our Lady identified herself by three names. She said, "I am the Immaculate Virgin" and, "I am the Mother of God, the Queen of Heaven." Two of these names, Immaculate Virgin and Queen of Heaven, will be addressed separately below. Of most significance was Our Lady's revelation under the same title, the Queen of Heaven, to both Adele and to Andree. Thus, the names of Mary show a parallelism and continuity between these two apparitions.

Queen of Heaven

On October 9, 1859, Adele Brise, advised by her parish priest, asked Our Lady to identify herself in God's Name, to which she responded, "I am the Queen of Heaven who prays for the conversion of sinners." Over seventy years later, Our Lady, in her departing words to Andree at Beauraing, said, "I am the Mother of God, the Queen of Heaven; pray always." Mary's identification as the Queen of Heaven to both Adele and Andree is unique, given that both share a Belgian heritage. What is the significance of this identification? Historically, when Belgium declared independence from the Netherlands in 1830, the government decided to establish a constitutional monarchy.[90] As a hereditary monarchy, succession to the throne passed through the royal family. The government appointed Leopold of Saxe-Coburg and Gotha as the first King of Belgium.[91] It would have been under Leopold I that the Brise family and many other Belgians decided

---

90 Cf. Emile Cammaerts, *Belgium: From the Roman Invasion to the Present Day* (Oakland: University of California Libraries, 1921), Chapter 24.

91 C.f. Henri Rolin, "The Constitutional Crisis in Belgium," *Foreign Affairs* 24.2, (Jan 1946), 300-3.

to come to America. Similarly, the monarchy continued through the time of the Beauraing apparitions and up until today.

Mary's identification as the Queen of Heaven emphasizes the eternal kingdom (heaven) over our temporal kingdom (earth). Mary was telling Adele that she was the Queen and that she wanted her and others to be members of the celestial court. As such, the Queen of Heaven title could also be seen as emphasizing that we should put no trust in princes (Ps 146:3) but instead put our trust in the Son of Man—Jesus.[92] Mary as the Queen of Heaven emphasizes that we as her children have a hereditary share in the eternal kingdom, if only we permit her to be our Queen so she may bring us to the King of kings.

Similarly, in Beauraing, Mary's identification as the Queen of Heaven was emphasizing the same ideas; namely, that the Belgian people must put their trust in Jesus. Given the spiritual apathy of the time, perhaps as a result of politics, Mary was

---

92 By this statement, I do not mean Our Lady was advocating for anarchy, but rather, that rulers of countries, because they are sinners, may not always have the eternal kingdom at the forefront of their decisions.

calling the people to return to the Lord. In addition, the Beauraing apparition came shortly before the Second World War. The Queen of Heaven appellation emphasizes that all temporal rulers receive their power from the King par excellence, whether they accept that claim or not. The temporal kings have the power to do good or to misuse their power. Mary's reminder of the eternal monarchy came at an appropriate time in which the Belgian immigrants and citizens could rediscover their citizenship of heaven as rightful heirs of the King of kings.

I Will Convert Sinners

In appearing to Adele, Our Lady identified who she was and her role in salvation by describing herself as the Queen of Heaven who prays for the conversion of sinners. In her departing words to Gilberte, Our Lady told her that she would convert sinners. We can see that Our Lady's language had changed. At Champion, she originally said she prays for conversions, but in Beauraing, she staunchly states she will convert sinners. Emil Neubert, SM, identified the work of Mary as a "Co-operatrix"[93]—one

---

[93] C.f. Emil Neubert, *My Ideal, Jesus, Son of Mary*

who works with Jesus in bringing about conversion, sanctification, and redemption.[94] Mary acknowledges her active role of prayer and work for conversions in cooperation with her Son's mission. Again, we can view the apparitions at Champion and Beauraing as complementary bookends. While in Champion, Adele cooperated in Our Lady's mission of praying and working for the conversion of sinners. Likewise, the prayers offered by the children of Beauraing as they heed Mary's instructions to pray always will assist her in her Co-operatrix role with her Son.

(Charlotte: TAN Books, 2010), 84. This short devotional book was written as instructions from Jesus and Mary for the laity and is based on the spirituality of Fr. William Joseph Chaminade, the founder of the Marianists. Emil Neubert also wrote on the mission of Mary which would complement this understanding of Mary working with her Son for the salvation of souls. See: Emil Neubert, *Mary's Apostolic Mission and Ours* (New Bedford, MA: Academy of the Immaculate, 2011).

94 C.f. Lumen Gentium 56-65. The Second Vatican Council's Dogmatic Constitution on the Church also expounds on this notion.

I Am the Immaculate Virgin

Besides Mary's identification as the Queen of Heaven to Andree, she also identified herself as the Immaculate Virgin. This name echoes Mary's earlier identification as the Immaculate Conception at Fatima, one who was preserved from original sin, but it also acknowledges that throughout her life, Mary remained sinless. The name is further intensified by what the children saw in a number of the apparitions: a golden heart.[95] The golden heart, coupled with Mary's identification as the Immaculate Virgin, results in a greater devotion to the Immaculate Heart. To have this devotion stem from the apparition is fitting, given that devotion to the Immaculate Heart was emphasized in the apparitions in Fatima and received by Lucia in the convent where the Five First Saturdays devotion was revealed. Mary's Immaculate Heart overflows with love for sinners, and her work of converting them flows from her love of God and love of her children. In addition, devotion to the Immaculate Heart was the fruit of Adele's apparition, as she received a picture of the Immaculate Heart to

---

95 The description of Mary's Golden Heart as seen by the children can be found in Beevers, 37-38.

enshrine in the chapels, commemorating the apparition site.[96] More importantly, the Beauraing apparitions are commonly known as "The Golden Heart." This name, unspoken but revealed within Mary's appearance, is similar to Champion since that apparition is also known by a devotional name rather than the identification of Mary to Adele. The names and roles attributed to Mary at the given apparitions parallel one another quite nicely and reveal Beauraing to be a continuation or a renewal of the message once spoken to a Belgian immigrant to the United States many years earlier.

Places of Pilgrimage

During several apparitions, including Lourdes and Fatima, Mary instructed the visionaries to ask the local bishop to build a chapel at the site of the apparition. This is notable because it again highlights Mary's desire to always bring people to her Son. The same was true at Beauraing—Our Lady said she desired a chapel to be built so that pilgrims could visit the site of her apparition. This request, however, was absent from the dialogue

---

96 C.f. Dominica, 9.

Adele had with Mary. Regardless of its absence, immediately following the apparition in Champion, chapels were indeed built, and eventually each chapel needed to be replaced to accommodate the growing numbers of visitors. The significance of Champion and Beauraing as places of pilgrimage rests with the fact that each played a pivotal role at specific moments in history. In 1871, the chapel became a refuge of prayer when people gathered there the night of the Peshtigo Fire. Their prayer at the site of Mary's apparition exemplified their trust and devotion to Our Lady, and as a result, their lives were spared. Just as those in the Belgian settlement flocked to the chapel that night, similarly on May 10, 1940

> German airplanes filled the skies over the eastern part of Belgium. . . . Bombs were dropped on cities and airports. . . . Panic swept the residents of Beauraing as the German troops approached. On May 11 most of the inhabitants packed their belongings and started toward the French border. They went on foot, on bicycle, by horse cart, and by automobile. German bombers roared overhead. Many of the people stopped at the hawthorn and light-

> ed vigil candles before they left the city. Beauraing was almost deserted. Only 129 people were left out of a population of two thousand.[97]

While the citizens of Beauraing did not take refuge at the hawthorn tree, they did, however, make a pious stop to ask the Virgin's intercession and protection during wartime. It was reported that the Rosary at Beauraing continued even with so few people in the town, illustrating the Queen of Heaven's continued intercession.[98] On September 7, 1944, when American tanks rolled into Beauraing, marking the end of the enemy occupation, the residents went to the apparition site to offer their gratitude to Mary.[99] Also signifying their gratitude, "twenty thousand freshly liberated prisoners of war made a pilgrimage to Beauraing on October 14, 1945, to thank the Virgin for their return to their homeland and their families."[100] The place of Mary's apparition was a place for prayers of intercession and thanksgiving during this turbu-

---

97 Debergh, 195-96.

98 Ibid., 196.

99 Ibid., 202.

100 Ibid.

lent time for the Belgian people. Individuals were able to take solace in their prayers at an apparition site. The same can be said of Champion; following the Peshtigo Fire, the annual celebration of the Assumption saw a significant increase in attendance from people who were just beginning to accept Adele's claims following that horrific event.[101] Both apparition sites, then, served as a place of refuge for those who wanted to exhibit their faith and devotion to Our Lord and Blessed Lady.

Banneux

Given the similarities of Champion and Beauraing, one would be remiss not to acknowledge the other approved apparition which occurred in Belgium several days following the conclusion of the Beauraing apparition. Beginning on January 15, 1933 and ending on March 2 of that same year, Our Lady appeared to a girl named Mariette Beco, who was eleven years old. The visionary's family situation was similar to that of the children at Beauraing and that of many within the settlement at Champion—"Her father [was] a hard working

101 Dominica, 32.

laborer and a badly-lapsed Catholic."[102] As a result of Mary's apparition, her father was reconciled with God through the sacrament of Penance. Mary's appearance in dress was similar to Champion, for Mariette saw a woman dressed in a long white robe which hung to her feet. Mary wore a blue girdle (instead of a yellow sash at Champion) and "rays of light shone from her head."[103] The apparition's message was also quite simple: Mary desired a chapel to be built and encouraged Mariette to pray hard. To those Belgians who saw Mary (and also in other apparitions), Our Lady emphasized the necessity of prayer. Our Lady identified herself as the Virgin of the Poor, and the spring of water at Banneux was set apart for all the nations but especially the sick, as Mary had come to relieve the sick.[104] The Banneux apparition, like Lourdes, involves a healing spring. But Mary's indication of her action or mission, that of relieving the physically sick, complements her primary mission of relieving the spiritually sick or infirm as indicated at Champion and Beauraing. Following the appari-

---

[102] Gillett, 260.

[103] Ibid., 263.

[104] Ibid., 264.

tion, a hospital was built at Banneux to fully carry out Mary's desire. This, of course, is similar to the chapel and convent built as a means for Adele to catechize the young people. As at Champion and Beauraing, Our Lady appeared at Banneux with a specific purpose: in this case to encourage a young girl to remain faithful to prayer and to establish a place of healing for the entire world.

Conclusion

The apparitions received by Adele, the five children at Beauraing, and Mariette at Banneux all reiterate the same message and desire of the Mary: to bring people closer to her Son. To the Belgian people, she appeared at appropriate times in which the faith needed to be renewed, and she appeared in similar places wearing similar attire. The messages and missions entrusted to the respective visionaries should not be seen in isolation from one another but as a continuation, renewal, and fulfillment of each another. It is appropriate that Adele's Mariophany was a bit more in-depth, for Adele was much older than the Beauraing children and Mariette. Reminding people of their heavenly destiny, Mary, she who is the Immaculate Virgin, the Golden Heart, the Queen of Heaven, and Virgin of the Poor, came to remind people that God exists and that they should live according to his commandments. Each apparition site has become a place of intercession in which the story of the respective vision may be passed on to future generations. Our Lady's message given to the Belgian people, first in the United States and then in Belgium itself, has relevance not only for them; it is for all times, all people, and all places.

Graces of Champion

On the properties of homeowners and churches throughout the area of Wisconsin where the Belgian immigrants settled, onlookers will find small little votive chapels (called Roadside Chapels). It was a custom of the Belgian people to establish small little chapels in the fields or at intersections for passersby to stop and pray for a short while. Often the chapels were built in gratitude to God for graces received. It could have been that their life was spared while drowning or after the delivery of several children. Each chapel has a story behind it.

At two of the parishes where I served, St. Peter and St. Hubert in Lincoln/Rosiere, roadside chapels could be found on the property; in Rosiere, it is dedicated to St. Peregrine, and in Lincoln, to Our Lady of the Afflicted. As the administrator of these parishes, I believed it was important to incorporate these devotional areas into the life of the Parish. During the summer of 2018, two parishioners were stricken with terminal cancer. One, a thirty-five-year-old son, brother, husband, and father, and the other an actively involved middle-aged woman in the parish. I planned special prayer vigils at these roadside chapels, gathering people to pray for a miracle. One of them, planned only forty-eight hours before, drew nearly one hundred people. Despite the successes of the prayer vigils in terms of turning out people to pray, I faced criticisms in comment boxes on social media promotion from individuals who said, "pray wherever you are." Essentially, they argued it didn't matter where you prayed, or if you prayed with others.

I agreed, if you couldn't join us, pray wherever you are. But the tenet expressed by these individuals is one I've heard for years, especially when I visit the shrines of the saints throughout the world. One person once remarked, "Do you really think it matters if you pray in Lisieux or Ars?" The answer is yes. I think it does matter. Because to each shrine, a special grace is accorded. This is something I encountered in the Schoenstatt movement as well. Another shrine in St. Augustine, Florida, dedicated to Our Lady of La Leche, is a place where couples struggling with infertility go and pray for the grace of a child. Many pilgrim couples eventually conceive or adopt a child. The grace of parenthood is strongly connected to the shrine. In the case of the roadside chapels at my churches, I believed that each chapel, because of its respective dedication to St. Peregrine or Our Lady of the Afflicted, potentially possessed the grace of healing for the sick. That's why I believed it was important to gather and pray, petitioning for a specific grace.

What about the National Shrine of Our Lady of Champion? What are the graces of the Champion shrine? I propose at the very least, three: conversion, catechesis, and healing.

Conversion

From the very identification and mission of Our Lady, it would seem that conversion should be one of the principal graces associated with the National Shrine of Our Lady of Champion. Mary revealed herself as the Queen of Heaven but also told us what she does as the Queen: she prays for the conversion of sinners. If this is what Mary does, then this special sanctuary should serve as a place where people pray for conversion. This conversion begins first with ourselves. Many people celebrate the sacrament of Reconciliation at the shrine, and as such, begin a movement toward personal conversion. When we celebrate the sacrament of Reconciliation, we pray the Act of Contrition, in which we resolve to avoid the near occasion of sin. This means that we take seriously the call for conversion. Ask Our Lady to pray for your conversion so that you might love God and leave behind sin. Pilgrims to the shrine also carry many of their family members in their hearts. Our Lady encouraged us to offer our Holy Communions for the conversion of sinners. While at the shrine, a pilgrim might pray for any number of people who are away from the sacraments, perhaps those within their own family, or their friends. Also, as we see a moral decline in society, the shrine can become a place where we pray for conversion in terms of advancing the gospel of life. Mary chose to reveal her identity and mission to Adele. One of the graces we can obtain by joining our prayers to those of Our Lady where she revealed herself is that of conversion.

Catechesis

Another grace one could perceive as associated with the National Shrine of Our Lady of Champion is the grace of catechesis. This was what Our Lady asked Adele to do: gather the children and teach them what they needed to know for salvation. The grace of catechesis came to its realization when Adele gathered like-minded women to join her in the mission. Today the grace of catechesis manifests itself in different ways. The first would be by the gathering of Catholic teachers, students, and religious education catechists for prayer at the shrine. In so doing, they dedicate themselves and seek the intercession of Mary to carry out the work she asked Adele to do, and now by extension, we continue to accomplish. Secondly, Mary spoke of teaching how to approach the sacraments. Through the work of shrine staff and volunteers, the grace of catechesis manifests itself when pilgrims are taught how to reverently receive the Holy Eucharist or how to worship the Lord in holy attire. At Champion, Mary revealed an active apostolate for Adele which consisted of teaching the faith. One of the graces associated with the shrine must be catechesis, by which conversion may also be attained.

Healing

A third grace accorded to the National Shrine of Our Lady of Champion, and a grace associated with many shrines dedicated to Mary or the saints, is that of healing. From the early days after the apparitions, people claimed healing. In a booklet published in 1950 by the Sisters of St. Francis of Bay Settlement, several cures are related.[105] Michael LaFond was a young crippled boy; nine women made a novena at the shrine with the child, and the boy left his crutches after the third visit. A young girl received the grace of healing of an open sore which closed after praying a novena at the shrine. A boy who never walked before was able to do so after praying at the shrine. A seventeen-year-old boy who contracted double pneumonia and pleurisy experienced an unexplainable healing after praying at the shrine. A pregnant woman with a serious kidney infection, bedridden for five weeks, experienced a change in her situation after nine people prayed a novena at the shrine for her. She delivered a healthy child. These are just a handful of healings that people claim to have received on account of their prayers at the National Shrine of Our Lady of Champion. Healings, physical, emotional, psychological, and spiritual, continue to occur today. As of this writing, no healing has been officially au-

---

[105] Page 32.

thenticated, but they are piously believed by those who received them and others.

The grace of healing should surprise no one familiar with religious shrines. Especially in the case of the Wisconsin apparition, Adele maintained a great concern for the sick. The day before her death, Adele told a former student, Josie, to "be kind to the sick and the old, and continue to instruct the children in their religion as I have done." The shrine continues the mission of Adele, of being kind to the sick as the shrine welcomes those who are in need of healing for special healing Masses and prayer services throughout the year. Through the intercession of Our Lady, and evident by the testimony of crutches left behind, and testimonies to this day, the grace of healing is alive and well at the National Shrine of Our Lady of Champion.

For What Grace Are You Praying?

As a pilgrim to the National Shrine of Our Lady of Champion, or as a devotee from afar, you should ask for what particular grace you are praying. Formulate your intention and be sure to leave it before the Blessed Sacrament and at the feet of Our Lady. After a pilgrimage, you might even consider what blessing or grace you have received as a result of your time of prayer. This grace might be evident immediately or will take time to manifest. When it does, you will know it was a grace of Champion, and then will be moved to thanksgiving.

What to Do When Visiting the Shrine

If you are planning your pilgrimage to the National Shrine of Our Lady of Champion, you won't want to miss out on the whole experience. It can be disappointing for a person to hear they missed one of the more important aspects of a shrine.

Visit the Welcome Center

The Welcome Center introduces a person to the history of the shrine. You can follow a timeline and understand the events throughout the shrine's lengthy history or see items of significance. Additionally, an informational video conveys history and allows you to learn the stories of fellow pilgrims of bygone years.

Celebrate the Sacraments

Confessions and Mass are celebrated daily. Anointing of the Sick is offered monthly. Many people find it appealing to celebrate the sacrament of Penance at a shrine because they are a passing pilgrim among many and not known to the priest as they might be in their home parish. Priests who hear confessions at the shrine hear thousands of confessions each year. Don't be embarrassed about your sins, there's a good chance he's heard it before, and confessing whatever is weighing on your soul will bring you much peace. Check the shrine's website or call ahead to confirm times. This prayer manual contains prayers before and after confession, along with a helpful examination of conscience. Additional prayers for before and after Mass and Anointing are included as well.

Pray in the Apparition Oratory

Below the Church is the Apparition Oratory. For decades, pilgrims have prayed in this place, believing it to be the location of the apparition. This prayer manual offers several different prayers to enhance your devotional time in this special spot.

Pray the Rosary, meditating on the mysteries intertwined with Our Lady's message and Adele's life. Begin one of the novenas there; pray the prayer before the statue of Our Lady of Grace, or offer the Litany of Our Lady of Champion. Spend a few moments in quiet prayer and reflection, conversing with Mary as your mother. She cares about what you have to say, listens to you, and prays for you.

Light a Candle

There are plenty of areas on the grounds to light votive candles. This is a popular custom at shrines throughout the world, and each shrine does it a bit differently. Look around and see all the candles that are lit. Remind yourself about all the pilgrims who have prayed in that spot before you and realize many will come after you. After you leave the shrine, your votive candle remains as a sign of your prayer continuing for days after your visit. Light a candle for the person for whom you are praying, for your children, or for yourself. If you want to let someone know you prayed for them, you can get a card from the gift store. This prayer manual provides a prayer for such an occasion.

Pray the Rosary

On the night of the Peshtigo Fire, local people gathered with Sister Adele and the school children and processed around the grounds with a statue of Mary and prayed the Rosary. In a similar fashion, you can walk the back grounds, going from rosary marker to rosary marker, reflecting on the Rosary mysteries. This prayer manual offers Rosary meditations which weave the story of the shrine into the mystery meditation.

Pray the Stations of the Cross

There are a few different opportunities on the shrine grounds to pray the Stations of the Cross. This prayer of the Church helps us remember the saving work of Christ. Each of the Station meditations in this prayer manual makes a connection to Adele, the apparition, or the shrine.

Visit Sister Adele's Grave

The shrine grounds contain a little cemetery in which Sister Adele is buried, alongside Sister Marguerite Allard, and a few others. Praying at the tombs of holy people dates back centuries. In

Rome, people pray in the catacombs, which are the tombs of the saints. To this day, many shrines have a special place where the individual is venerated. Pray for Sister Adele, and all buried in the cemetery. This prayer manual suggests a prayer for your visit.

Pray at the Various Grottos

Even though the shrine property is small in comparison to other shrines throughout the world, there are several grottos to Our Lady of Grace, Our Lady of Lourdes, Our Lady of Fatima, and St. Francis. Instead of just walking by the grotto and thinking about how pretty it is, spend some time in prayer before the statues of Our Lady or the saints. A pilgrimage is a time of prayer and an opportunity to engage our spiritual senses. What we see can bring us to a point of prayer. You may even wish to sit down for a few moments and journal about your experience at the shrine. This prayer manual provides prayers to be prayed at each grotto. When we pray, God bestows grace upon us. Don't miss the opportunity.

Visit the Gift Store

Mother Angelica always spoke about holy reminders, and maybe you would like a holy reminder of this pilgrimage: a statue, medal, rosary, or some other item related to the shrine. Additionally, the shrine gift store is a comprehensive Catholic gift shop with many Catholic books and other devotional items. It's a great place to do your shopping for First Communion or Confirmation, or to find a small gift to help someone fall in love with Jesus again. Not only will you or someone you love benefit from your purchase, but you will also be helping to support the work of the shrine.

Visit the School House Café

If you need a bite to eat or something to drink, the School House Café, located in the 1885 building, will be able to satiate your hunger or quench your thirst. Grab a bite to eat, have a drink of java, see the historic photos, and catch up on your miniature catechism lesson.

Other Places of Interest While on Pilgrimage

The greater Green Bay area offers many different places to visit. Some are connected to the shrine, others to Belgian heritage, and others to the cultural climate of Wisconsin. If you have time, you might wish to check out the following places.

Peshtigo Fire Museum: Located in Peshtigo, Wisconsin, forty-five minutes from the National Shrine of Our Lady of Champion. You will learn more about the history of the Peshtigo Fire which threatened the shrine property and see the tabernacle that was spared. Be sure to check their website or call ahead because they have seasonal hours.

Belgian Heritage Center: Located in Namur, Wisconsin, the Belgian Heritage Center is the former St. Mary of the Snows, Church. This location is also the historic foundation of the Norbertine order that came from Berne Abbey to nurture the faith of the people along the peninsula. There you can learn about Belgian culture and traditions. Check their website or call ahead to learn their hours.

Area roadside chapels: Besides the roadside chapel located on the National Shrine of Our Lady of Champion property, many roadside chapels were built throughout the peninsula. Sometimes they were built in gratitude for a grace received, such as good health or deliverance from drowning. There are several dozen roadside chapels throughout the area. Find a brochure at the shrine or at the Belgian Heritage Center and pray in these votive chapels where families and neighbors have prayed for decades.

National Shrine of St. Joseph at the St. Norbert College: The National Shrine of St. Joseph fosters devotion to the foster-father of Jesus. Visit the chapel on the campus of St. Norbert and seek the intercession of the patron of the universal Church and a holy death.

St. Norbert Abbey: Located in DePere, Wisconsin, is the home of the Norbertine Order. Join them for Mass or participate in sung Liturgy of the Hours.

St. Francis Xavier Cathedral is the mother church of the Diocese of Green Bay and is adorned with beautiful murals, including one of the crucifixion. Beautiful stained glass windows and statuary enhance one's prayer and meditation in this sacred place. When you are there, don't forget to walk to the nearby Cathedral Book & Gift shop.

Lambeau Field: Often called in jest the second cathedral or basilica in Green Bay, it is one of the most historic football stadiums of the NFL. The Packers are a homegrown team, with the unique feature of being owned by its fans who can have shares of stock. The Packers have had a long history with Catholicism, from Vince Lombardi practicing his faith at St. Willebrord in downtown Green Bay to the summer training camp at St. Norbert College to the annual Bishop's Charity Game. While you are in town, it might be a must see for the football loving fan.

Other Marian Shrines in Wisconsin

Our Lady of Guadalupe, La Crosse: A beautiful church situated in the bluffs of La Crosse celebrates a beautiful liturgy and fosters devotion to Our Lady of Guadalupe. Pray at the grotto for the unborn or at the areas with beautiful paintings of the saints.

National Shrine of Mary, Help of Christians (Holy Hill) Hubertus, Wisconsin, is in a picturesque area of Wisconsin and provides many opportunities for prayer in the upper basilica, in the St. Therese chapel, in the Our Lady, Help of Christians devotional area, or the outdoor stations and other grottos. During certain months, the scenic tower is open for viewing the beautiful surroundings.

Part II

Prayers and Devotions

Preparation for Receiving the Sacraments

When individuals plan their pilgrimage to the National Shrine of Our Lady of Champion, they often choose to celebrate the sacraments. Mass and confessions are offered daily, and the Anointing of the Sick is offered on a monthly basis.

The sacraments, specifically confession and the Eucharist, were essential to the message received by Adele Brise. Mary instructed Adele to make a general confession, offer her communion for the conversion of sinners, and teach the children how to approach the sacraments. At the end of Adele's life, she told her friend Josie to be kind to the sick and the old. Given the testimonies of those who are believed to have been healed through Our Lady's intercession and Adele's concern for the sick, those who are ill might receive the Anointing of the Sick while at the shrine.

One of the ways we can fulfill Our Lady's request of Adele is to properly approach the sacraments. How do you prepare for the sacraments? How do you pray before and after? There are traditional prayers to pray before and after going to confession or receiving the Eucharist at Mass. Such prayers are one way we prepare to approach and receive the sacraments.

Celebrating the Sacrament of Reconciliation

Prayer Before Confession

Dear Lord Jesus, you were born of the Blessed Virgin Mary to be the Savior and Redeemer of the world. I acknowledge before you today that I am a sinner in need of forgiveness and healing. Help me to examine my conscience thoroughly so that I may know my sins and confess them in their entirety. I wish to leave no stone unturned, no sin unconfessed. Calm my fears and worries about confession and give me peace in my soul as I approach your throne of mercy. Amen.

Act of Contrition

O my God, I am heartily sorry for having offended you, and I detest all my sins because of your just punishments, but most of all because they offend you, my God, who are all good and deserving of all my love. I firmly resolve with the help of your grace to sin no more and to avoid the near occasion of sin. Amen.

Prayer After Confession

Thank you, Lord, for your mercy, for the forgiveness you extend to me each time I come before you. I thank you for the ministry of your priest, whom you called to serve in persona Christi, upon whom you have bestowed the power to forgive sins, as you did to the apostles when you told them, whoever's sins you forgive, they are forgiven. Give to your priest many graces for his ministry as he continues your ministry today. As I go forward now, cleansed of sin, help me to never fall into the same sins of my past life; may I run far away from the near occasion of sin. Allow me to remain in your grace today, tomorrow, and everyday of my life. Amen.

How to Make A Good Confession

Adapted from Confession Its Fruitful Practice

I. The Examination of Conscience

A. Beginning Prayer

O God, Father of Light, who enlightenest everyone that comes into this world, give me light, love and sorrow, that I may discover, detest and confess all the sins I have committed. O Holy Ghost, Spirit of Love and Dispenser of all graces, help me to receive this great sacrament worthily; give me Thy grace that I may make a careful examination of conscience and discover my sins; touch my heart that I may hate and detest them, and assist me to make a firm resolution to avoid sin henceforth. Spirit of Love and Truth, assist me to make a sincere, entire and truthful Confession to Thy representative, the priest, and thus obtain Thy forgiveness, Thy grace and Thy love. O Jesus, my Redeemer, through Thy most holy merits, grant me the grace of heartfelt contrition and amendment of life. To Thee I look for the grace to make this Confession well, that I may glorify Thee. O most holy Virgin Mary, Mother of my Saviour, and my own most loving Mother, thou who art so compassionate towards those who desire to repent, help me to call to mind all my offenses and to be truly sorry for having offended God. My dear Guardian Angel, who hast been a witness of my sins, help me now to recall them and to be truly sorry for them. All you Saints and Angels of Heaven, pray for me that I may now bring forth fruits worthy of penance. Amen.

B. Points for the Examination of Conscience

When did I make my last Confession? Did I have true sorrow? Did I conceal any mortal sin and thus commit a sacrilege? Did I receive Holy Communion after a bad Confession? Did I receive Holy Communion while in the state of mortal sin? How many times have I received the sacraments unworthily? Did I forget a mortal sin in my last Confession? (It must be confessed in this Confession.) Did I perform my penance? Did I make necessary restitution? Did I repair injury done to another's good name? Have I tried to avoid the near occasions of sin?

1. The Ten Commandments of God

1. I am the Lord, thy God: thou shalt not have strange gods before Me.

Have I: Denied my religion? Spoken against it or its ministers? Doubted any article of Faith? Affiliated myself with a forbidden secret society? Read books, papers, etc., belittling morality, scoffing at virtue or causing doubts regarding the Church's teachings? Despaired of, or presumed on God's mercy by continuing a long time in prayers, fortune-telling, spiritism, the Ouija board, etc.? Complained or murmured against God or His Providence? Refused to resign myself to His Will? Neglected daily prayers? Or said them carelessly, with willful distractions? Shown irreverence towards the Blessed Sacrament, or in the use of sacramentals: holy water, the Sign of the Cross, etc.? Used words of Scripture in jest? Failed to keep promises or vows made to God?

2. Thou shalt not take the Name of the Lord, thy God, in vain.

Have I: Used the Name of God or of Jesus in cursing? In swearing? In jest? Have I done this from habit? Have I been guilty of blasphemous thoughts, words, or writings? Desired evil to others, or cursed them? Asked God to curse them? Encouraged others to use evil or profane language?

3. Remember thou keep holy the Sabbath day (Sunday).

Have I: Willfully missed Mass on Sundays or Holy days of Obligation? Come late through my own fault and missed a considerable part of the Mass? Misbehaved in church? Caused others to do so? Performed unnecessary servile work for a considerable time on such days (more than 2 or 3 hours)? Desecrated them by excessive drinking or gambling, or by keeping sinful company or frequenting sinful amusements?

4. Honor thy Father and thy Mother.

Children

Have I: Been disobedient, ungrateful or stubborn toward my parents, teachers or pastors? Wished serious harm to parents or wished they were dead? Used insulting language toward them? Struck them in resentment or bad will? Made them unhappy by misconduct? Disobeyed when they forbade going with bad companions, to bad shows, or other dangerous places? Failed to assist them when they needed help in old age, sickness, or poverty? Failed to carry out their last will? Neglected to pray for the repose of their souls? Have I broken any civil laws? Have I disobeyed any lawful authority?

Employees

Have I: Failed to carry out the commands of my employer? Fomented discord? Failed in respect or honesty?

5. Thou shalt not kill. (This includes also injury to the soul and uncharitableness.)

Have I: By act, participation, instigation, counsel, or consent, been guilty of anyone's death, or bodily injury? Or of destroying the life of the unborn? Have I desired another's death, or wished misfortune to him? Given way to anger and passion? Ill-treated others? Been at enmity with others? Refused to speak to them? Willfully entertained thoughts of hatred, revenge, jealousy, aversion, resentment, or contempt for others? Provoked others to anger? Harmed the souls of others by giving scandal or throwing temptation in their way? Given in to moods of sullenness and moroseness? Shown sensitiveness and hurt feelings over trifling matters? Approved or encouraged the anger of others? Attempted suicide or entertained thoughts of it? Participated in or consented to "mercy killing"? Sinned by excessive eating and/or drinking? Become intoxicated? Sinned by abusing drugs? Has anyone through my fault died without having the priest and religious ministrations? Have I sent or advised parents to send children to a school where their Catholic faith or morals would be endangered?

6. Thou shalt not commit adultery. 9. Thou shalt not covet thy neighbor's wife.

Have I: Committed impure acts? Alone, or with another? With a single or married person? Of my own or the opposite sex? With a relative? Dwelt with pleasure on impure thoughts and imaginations? Or consented to them in my heart? Willfully desired to see or do anything impure? Used impure language, allusions, words of double meaning? How many were listening? Have I listened with willful pleasure to immodest language? Sung or listened to improper songs? Sinned by impure or immodest touch or action, with myself, or with others? Boasted of my sins? Read immoral books? Loaned or sold them to others? Written improper things? Gazed with willful pleasure on improper objects or pictures, or shown them to others? Voluntarily exposed myself to temptation by curiosity? By frequenting dangerous company or places? By sinful amusements? By immodest dances? By watching indecent plays or movies? Been guilty of undue familiarities or sinful kisses? Kept company with a married person? Am I keeping sinful company now? Have I dressed immodestly? Have I by immodest dress or freedom of speech or manners been a cause of temptation to the purity of others? Have I deliberately led others into sin? Or taken part in their sins? (The circumstances which change the nature of a sin, such as whether married or single, gender, if related, etc., must be mentioned in confessing these sins.) Have I been guilty of sins contrary to marriage obligations? Have I used contraceptives or abortifacient "contraceptives" or been sterilized? Encouraged, advised, or instructed others to commit such sins? Failed to train my children in matters of chastity?

7. Thou shalt not steal. 10. Thou shalt not covet thy neighbor's goods.

Have I: Stolen money? How much? Stolen other goods? From whom (poor, rich, Church, parents)?

Have I returned the stolen goods or their value? Knowingly bought or accepted stolen goods? Damaged another's property in any way? Neglected to pay for such damage? Refused to give back borrowed things? Kept things that were found without making sufficient effort to find the owner? Cheated? Passed worthless money? Performed work carelessly? Wasted time at work? Squandered my property? Wronged my family by prodigal expenses, such as excessive drinking, gambling, etc.? Sought the things of this world too eagerly? Desired to steal or commit any injustice? Been a party to another's stealing or injustice? Shared in or concealed stolen goods?

8. Thou shalt not bear false witness against thy neighbor.

Have I: Given false evidence in a court of justice? Deliberately told a lie to deceive another? Told lies which caused injury to another's reputation and good name? (This is the sin of calumny.) Made known the true but secret faults of others without necessity? (This is the sin of detraction.) Listened to such speech? Caused ill feeling by tale-bearing? Judged others rashly or suspected them rashly? Read others' letters and violated their right to certain secrets? Been guilty in any other way of uncharitable speech? Have I neglected to repair the harm done by my sinful speech? Have I spoken against a priest, or anyone consecrated to God? (This is a sacrilege.) Have I flattered others in their sins and bad habits? Have I sinned by hypocrisy and pretense of virtue? Signed false papers or documents? Have I attributed bad motives to others when I could not be certain of their motive?

Celebrating the Eucharist

Prayers Before Receiving Communion

Prayer of St. Ambrose

Lord, Jesus Christ, I approach your banquet table in fear and trembling, for I am a sinner, and dare not rely on my own worth but only on your goodness and mercy. I am defiled by many sins in body and soul, and by my unguarded thoughts and words. Gracious God of majesty and awe, I seek your protection, I look for your healing, poor troubled sinner that I am, I appeal to you, the fountain of all mercy. I cannot bear your judgment, but I trust in your salvation. Lord, I show my wounds to you and uncover my shame before you. I know my sins are many and great, and they fill me with fear, but I hope in your mercies, for they cannot be numbered. Lord Jesus Christ, eternal King, God and man, crucified for mankind, look upon me with mercy and hear my prayer, for I trust in you. Have mercy on me, full of sorrow and sin, for the depth of your compassion never ends. Praise to you, saving sacrifice, offered on the wood of the cross for me and for all mankind. Praise to the noble and precious blood, flowing from the wounds of my crucified Lord Jesus Christ and washing away the sins of the whole world. Remember, Lord, your creature, whom you have redeemed with your blood. I repent my sins, and I long to put right what I have done. Merciful Father, take away all my offenses and sins; purify me in body and soul, and make me worthy to taste the holy of holies. May your body and blood, which I intend to receive, although I am unworthy, be for me the remission of my sins, the washing away of my guilt, the end of my evil thoughts, and the rebirth of my better instincts. May it incite me to do the works pleasing to you and profitable to my health in body and soul, and be a firm defense against the wiles of my enemies. Amen.

Prayer of St. Thomas Aquinas

Almighty and ever-living God, I approach the sacrament of your only-begotten Son, our Lord Jesus Christ. I come sick to the doctor of life, unclean to the fountain of mercy, blind to the radiance of eternal light, and poor and needy to the Lord of heaven and earth.

O my God I am heartily sorry for having offended Thee and I detest all of my sins because of thy just punishments but most of all because they offend Thee, my God, who art all good and worthy of all my love. I firmly resolve with the help of thy grace to sin no more and to avoid the near occasion of sin. Amen.

Act of Faith (Traditional)

O my God, I firmly believe that you are one God in three divine Persons, Father, Son, and Holy Spirit. I believe that your divine Son became man and died for our sins, and that he will come to judge the living and the dead. I believe these and all the truths which the holy Catholic Church teaches, because you have revealed them, who can neither deceive nor be deceived. Amen.

Prayers After Communion

Anima Christi

Soul of Christ, sanctify me.
Body of Christ, save me.
Blood of Christ, inebriate me.
Water from the side of Christ, wash me.
Passion of Christ, strengthen me.
O good Jesus, hear me.
Within Thy wounds hide me.
Suffer me not to be separated from Thee.
From the malignant enemy, defend me.
In the hour of my death, call me.
And bid me come to Thee.
That with Thy saints I may praise Thee.

Prayer of St. Bonaventure

Pierce, O my sweet Lord Jesus, my inmost soul with the most joyous and healthful wound of your love, with true serene and most holy apostolic charity, that my soul may ever languish and melt with love and longing for you, that it may yearn for you and faint for your courts, and long to be dissolved and to be with you. Grant that my soul may hunger after you, the bread of angels, the refreshment of holy souls, our daily and supernatural bread, having all sweetness and savor and every delight of taste; let my heart hunger after and feed upon you, upon whom the angels desire to look, and may my inmost soul be filled with the sweetness of your savor; may it ever thirst after you, the fountain of life, the fountain of wisdom and knowledge, the fountain of eternal light, the torrent of pleasure, the richness of the house of God; may it ever compass you, seek you, find you, run to you, attain you, meditate upon you, speak of you and do all things to the praise and glory of your name, with humility and discretion, with love and delight, with ease and affection, and with perseverance unto the end; may you alone be ever my hope, my entire assistance, my riches, my delight, my pleasure, my joy, my rest and tranquility, my peace, my sweetness, my fragrance, my sweet savor, my food, my refreshment, my refuge, my help, my wisdom, my portion, my possession and my treasure, in whom may my mind and my heart be fixed and firm and rooted immovably, henceforth and forever. Amen.

Prayer After Communion for the Conversion of Sinners

Eternal Father, I kneel before you this day with a grateful heart because you have allowed me to receive the body and blood of your son, Jesus, in Holy Communion.

Thank you for sending the Queen of Heaven to earth with a message calling us to conversion and emphasizing the sacraments. For when she appeared to Adele Brise in 1859, she asked her to offer her Holy Communion for the conversion of sinners. Just as Adele did long ago, I wish to do likewise this day.

I offer to you, Eternal Father, the body, blood, soul, and divinity of your Son for the conversion of sinners, including myself, in reparation for sin, and the salvation of souls and *(pause to name specific individual/group)*.

Through Our Lady's maternal solicitude, may the hearts of hardened sinners return to the sacraments of Penance and Eucharist, especially to Sunday Mass and to daily prayer. As I go forward from this holy Mass, help me to fear nothing, knowing that you are with me and are always guiding me and that Our Lady constantly intercedes for me.

Make me aware of your presence this day and always. Amen.

Celebrating the Anointing of the Sick

Prayer Before Receiving the Anointing of the Sick

Dear Lord Jesus, I present myself to you this day. I come to you like the blind man on the side of the road, like the paralytic man who was lowered down from the roof, like the hemorrhaging woman. I approach you in faith and confidence that you are the Divine Physician, and that you have power over disease and sickness. Open my mind, my heart, my body, and my soul to receive your healing grace, as your priest lays hands and anoints me in your sacred name. I resign myself to your Holy Will, knowing that your ways are better than my ways. In your healing name, I pray. Amen.

Prayer After Receiving the Anointing of the Sick

Thank you, Jesus, for the sacramental graces conferred upon me through the sacrament of the Anointing of the Sick. May they sustain me through my illness (or my surgery and recovery). Blessed Mary, Health of the Sick, you revealed your concern for the sick in Lourdes with a miraculous spring of healing water; throughout the ages many people have called upon your intercession. Intercede for me now, and ask Jesus to show me His healing mercy. I place my confidence and trust in your intercession, and in our Lord, Savior, and Healer, Jesus Christ. Amen.

Praying the Rosary With Sister Adele[106]

The rosary remains one of the most popular forms of Marian devotion for Catholics today. Many pilgrims pray the Rosary while visiting the Shrine. For some, it might be a daily devotion, or for others, a prayer recited on special occasions or when a need is great. On the night of the Peshtigo Fire on October 8, 1871, local townspeople gathered at the then Chapel of Our Lady of Good Help. They joined Sister Adele, the other sisters, and children in prayer, as the fire ravaged the land and they stared death in the eye. They prayed the Rosary while processing around the grounds, turning in a different direction when the smoke became too

---

[106] Those familiar with Fr. Looney's writings might recognize that this was a former book. The meditations for each mystery have been re-written, representing the development of thought and devotion from 2012 to 2018.

much. On the morning of October 9, 1871, twelve years to the day that Mary appeared to Adele, the fire passed over the property and their lives were spared. Each year, to commemorate the "Miracle" of the Fire, a candlelit rosary procession re-enacts the events of the night. Rosary markers on the grounds of the National Shrine of Our Lady of Champion allow pilgrims to take in the beauty of the property and pray the Rosary outside. Other pilgrims pray the Rosary in the Apparition Oratory or in the Apparition Chapel.

The following Rosary reflections help a pilgrim, whether on the grounds or in their home, to pray the Rosary and learn about Adele Brises' life and the message she received from the Queen of Heaven. As you pray the words of the Hail Mary, "pray for us sinners," remember that you are joining Mary in her mission as she revealed to Adele that as the Queen of Heaven she prays for the conversion of sinners. Allow your Rosary to participate in Mary's prayer and fulfill her request for us to join her in that prayer.

How to Pray the Rosary

The Apostles' Creed

I believe in God, the Father Almighty, Creator of heaven and earth; and in Jesus Christ, His only Son, our Lord, who was conceived by the Holy Spirit, born of the Virgin Mary, suffered under Pontius Pilate, was crucified, died, and was buried. He descended into hell; the third day He arose from the dead. He ascended into heaven, and is seated at the right hand of God, the Father Almighty, from thence He shall come to judge the living and the dead.

I believe in the Holy Spirit, the Holy Catholic Church, the communion of saints, the forgiveness of sins, the resurrection of the body, and the life everlasting. Amen.

The Our Father

Our Father, who art in heaven, hallowed be Thy name; Thy kingdom come; Thy will be done on earth as it is in heaven.

Give us this day our daily bread; and forgive us our trespasses as we forgive those who trespass against us; and lead us not into temptation but deliver us from evil. Amen.

The Hail Mary

Hail Mary, full of grace, the Lord is with thee, blessed art thou amongst women and blessed is the fruit of thy womb, Jesus.

Holy Mary, Mother of God, pray for us sinners now and at the hour of our death. Amen.

The Glory Be

Glory be to the Father, and to the Son, and to the Holy Spirit.

As it was in the beginning, is now, and ever shall be, world without end. Amen.

The Fatima Prayer

Oh my Jesus, forgive us our sins. Save us from the fires of hell. Lead all souls to Heaven, especially those in most need of Thy mercy.

Hail, Holy Queen

Hail, holy Queen, Mother of Mercy; our life, our sweetness and our hope. To thee do we cry, poor banished children of Eve. To thee do we send up our sighs, mourning and weeping in this valley of tears. Turn then, most gracious Advocate, thine eyes of mercy toward us. And after this our exile, show unto us the blessed fruit of Thy womb, Jesus. O clement, O loving, O sweet Virgin Mary. Pray for us, O Holy Mother of God, that we may be made worthy of the promises of Christ. Amen.

Joyful Mysteries

Traditionally prayed on Mondays and Saturdays

Annunciation: The angel Gabriel visits Nazareth and Mary receives her vocation to be the mother of our God, Lord, and Savior. In this mystery, we recall how Mary appeared to Adele and invited her to a missionary vocation of teaching children and preparing them for the sacraments. Mary, pray for us as we discern and live our vocations. May we always be faithful and ready to serve as you did.

Visitation: After hearing that her cousin Elizabeth was with child, Mary set out in haste to visit, spend time with her, and help her during the last months of her pregnancy. Mary visits Elizabeth's home and remains with her three months. In this mystery we recall how Mary visited Adele in 1859 on three occasions and how Adele visited the homes of strangers after the apparition and stayed with them for a short while to teach the faith, and in exchange, serve the household by doing various chores. Mary, pray for us that we may be effective evangelizers and missionaries like you.

Nativity of Jesus: Joseph and Mary travel to Bethlehem, and it is there, in a stable, that the Son of God was born, placed in a manger, and adored by His parents, shepherds, and wisemen. In this mystery we recall Mary's words to Adele to teach the children what they need to know for salvation. Mary, pray for us that we might personally know Jesus who was born for us as our Savior in Bethlehem.

Presentation: Joseph and Mary bring Jesus to the temple and make their offering of two turtle doves. Once Simeon takes the Christ child into his arms, he realizes the fulfillment of his life's mission. In this mystery, we recall how Adele would present the children she prepared for First Holy

Communion to the priest for admittance to the sacraments. Through Mary's intercession, may we always present ourselves worthily before the Lord.

Finding of Jesus in the Temple: After making their pilgrimage to Jerusalem for the annual festival, Joseph and Mary journey back to their home, and along the way notice they cannot find Jesus among the caravan. They return to Jerusalem and search for him, only to find him among the Teachers in the temple. In this mystery, we recall how many souls are lost right now, having turned their backs on God and rejected His teachings. Through Mary's intercession, may these lost souls find themselves once again among the assembly of believers, worshipping God each week and praying daily.

Luminous Mysteries

Traditionally prayed on Thursdays

Baptism of the Lord: John the Baptist was at the river Jordan when the one whose sandal he is not worthy to untie presents Himself and wishes to enter the water. The Trinity is present, as the voice of the Father is heard telling us that Jesus is His beloved Son and the presence of the Holy Spirit in the form of a dove hovers nearby. In this mystery, we recall how Mary told Adele to teach the children how to make the Sign of the Cross. The same cross traced on our foreheads and the invocation of the Trinity pronounced as water was poured over our heads. Mary, please pray for us, that we will remain faithful to our baptismal promises.

Wedding Feast of Cana: The evangelist John tells us that Mary was at this wedding feast and played an important role in the miracle of Cana. Jesus listens to His mother and her request, and acts upon it. In this mystery we recall the words Mary spoke to Adele, her invitation to prayer and evangelization. We listen to those words and strive to live them in our lives. As Mary saw the immediate need of the wedding couple, we ask her now to intercede for us and be attentive to our needs and prayers, obtaining for us all that we need while on our earthly pilgrimage.

Proclamation of the Kingdom: At the very beginning of Jesus' ministry, He proclaimed that the Kingdom of Heaven was at hand. His parables revealed the depths of the Kingdom of Heaven. His teachings show us the way to the Father's House.

In this mystery we recall the missionary work of Adele, and how she went door to door proclaiming Jesus as Lord and sharing His teachings. Through Mary's intercession, may we be given the same missionary zeal as Adele, and be emboldened to proclaim the Gospel to our family, friends, and all we meet.

Transfiguration: Jesus took three of the apostles, Peter, James, and John, up the mountain, and there they experience this heavenly exchange between Jesus, Moses, and Elijah. In this mystery we recall in the pages of the scriptures these Old Testament figures who appeared to Jesus, and now Almighty God has chosen to send His mother to earth with messages for these visionaries. Adele was privileged to see the grandeur of Heaven in that visitation of Mary. Mother Mary, please pray for us so that one day we too might see our heavenly homeland and make our home there for all eternity.

Institution of the Eucharist: On the night before He died, Jesus celebrated the Passover with His disciples, and during that meal took bread and wine, saying, "This is my Body," and, "This is my blood." In this mystery we recall Mary's request of

Adele to offer her Holy Communion for the conversion of sinners and how Adele prepared the children for First Holy Communion. Mary, obtain for us a deeper appreciation for the Eucharist we celebrate day after day and week after week.

Sorrowful Mysteries

Traditionally prayed on Tuesdays and Fridays

Agony in the Garden: While Jesus prayed in the garden, His disciples were nearby, falling asleep. Jesus asks them, "Could you not keep watch with me for one hour?" In this mystery, we recall Our Lady's question to Adele: "Why are you standing here in idleness while your companions are working in the vineyard of the Lord?" Adele had fallen asleep in her mission and Our Lady came to awaken it within her soul. Dear Blessed Mother, please pray for us, that we might always be vigilant in keeping watch with the Lord and doing His will.

Scourging at the Pillar: Jesus was tortured and beaten, whipped and scourged. He bled for our offenses. In this mystery we recall Adele's physical limitations, infirmities, and sufferings, and how she patiently endured them, uniting them to the suffering of Christ. Mary, please pray for me, that I may suffer without complaint.

Crowning with Thorns: A crown of thorns was placed on Jesus' head and bystanders mockingly hailed Him as the King of the Jews. We know that Jesus is King of kings, Lord of lords, and King of the Universe. In this mystery we recall how every King needs a Queen, and how Mary revealed this identity to Adele, "I am the Queen of Heaven, who prays for the conversion of sinners." Mary, please pray for us, and inspire us to make reparation for the sins of the world.

Carrying of the Cross: Sentenced to death on a cross, Jesus picks up his cross, and begins the Way of the Cross. He fell three times, met His mother along the way, consoled the women of Jerusalem, and was helped by Simon of Cyrene. He is stripped of his garments and nailed to the cross. In this mystery, we recall the suffering, persecution, embarrassment, and betrayal Adele endured as she carried out her mission. Blessed Mother, please pray for me, that as I carry the crosses of my life, I may remain faithful in times of struggle.

Crucifixion: Jesus hung on the cross for three hours until He breathed His last. He prayed from the cross, forgave his persecutors, promised eternal life to the Good Thief, and entrusted His mother to the care of John. In this mystery we recall how Adele worked to satisfy Jesus' thirst for souls and helped others to take Mary into their homes. Blessed Mother, please pray for us that we might forgive others, love you as our mother, and that at the hour of our death we may inherit the gift of eternal life.

Glorious Mysteries

Traditionally prayed on Wednesdays and Sundays

Resurrection: On the first day of the week, Mary Magdalene went to the tomb in order to mourn at Jesus' tomb. Upon her arrival she discovers the tomb empty and converses with Jesus. She immediately brings the Good News to the apostles, two of whom sprint to the tomb to see for themselves. Jesus appeared to the disciples for forty days until his Ascension. In this mystery we recall how Adele shared the Good News of salvation with those she met. Dear Blessed Mother, please pray for us, that we might be messengers of the Good News in our world.

Ascension: Forty days after Jesus rose from the dead, he climbed the Mount and ascended before the sight of His mother and apostles. Before leaving, He instructed them to go and make disciples of all nations. In this mystery, we recall Mary's exhortation to Adele: "Go, and fear nothing." Blessed Mother, please pray for us, that we always remember that Christ has commissioned us both to be His disciples and to make disciples of others.

Descent of the Holy Spirit: Mary persevered with the disciples in prayer while in the Upper Room waiting for the coming of the promised Holy Spirit. In this mystery we recall the gifts of the Spirit received at Baptism and stirred aflame in Confirmation. Blessed Mother, please pray for us, that we might use the gifts we have received and manifest the fruits of the Spirit in our daily life.

Assumption: At the completion of her earthly life, God chose to take His mother Mary, body and soul, into heavenly glory. In this mystery, we recall the importance of the Assumption feast day as a Pilgrimage day. Blessed Mother, please pray for us, that our devotion to you as our mother may grow day by day.

Coronation: In biblical times, the Queen was always the mother of the King. Since Jesus is the King of the Universe, it is only fitting that He should choose to crown His mother. Mary's apparition to Adele confirms this, as she revealed herself as the Queen of Heaven. Mother Mary, be our advocate and intercessor before the throne of your Son. Bring our petitions, concerns, and struggles before Him.

The Stations of the Cross

Introduction

For centuries, pilgrims have journeyed to the Holy Land, especially to Jerusalem, and have walked the *Via Dolorosa*, the Way of the Cross. In one sense, it is a pilgrimage within a pilgrimage. The Stations of the Cross are precisely that, a pilgrimage, journeying from one station to the next, contemplating Jesus's pilgrimage to Calvary and entering into prayer and dialogue with our Savior.

For many people, the Stations of the Cross are a Lenten devotion. Parishes schedule times for this devotion. The Stations can be prayed throughout the year. As people make their own pilgrimages to shrines, they spend a significant time in prayer and reflection. A pilgrimage is an opportunity for devotion, to engage the spiritual life, and deepen one's prayer and meditation. In addition to celebrating the sacraments and praying the Rosary, pilgrims may wish to pray the Stations of the Cross.

At the National Shrine of Our Lady of Champion, there are a few options to pray the Stations of the Cross. During the winter months, it might be more comfortable to pray the stations located inside the church. During the summer and autumn, the outdoor stations provide a beautiful meditative experience in the beauty of this "wild country." These meditations for the stations incorporate Our Lady's message and Adele's life within the passion of Jesus Christ.

Prayer Before the Stations

I desire now to journey with you Lord Jesus to the hill of Calvary. As I meditate and see in my mind's eye all that you endured for my salvation, as I listen to the message of Our Lady, and am inspired by the life of Adele Brise, allow me to experience a profound conversion of heart, an aversion for sin, and a deep love for you and the Church.

1. Pilate Condemns Jesus to Die

V. We adore you O Christ and we bless you.
R. Because by your Holy Cross you have redeemed the world.

After being betrayed by the kiss of Judas, Jesus is brought before Pilate, who asks Him, "What is truth?" Jesus remains silent, because He is THE TRUTH. Pilate then led Jesus before the crowd, saying, "Behold, the man." The crowd shouted, "Crucify Him." And with that, Jesus receives His condemnation of death and begins His Way of the Cross.

When Mary appeared to Adele, she instructed her to teach the children what they needed to know for salvation. Mary wants us to know Jesus as the Truth. She wants us to know Jesus' teachings as Truth.

As we journey this Way of the Cross, let us behold Jesus for who He is, our Savior and Redeemer. Mary, my mother, intercede for us, so that we might believe and know the Truth.

2. Jesus Accepts His Cross

V. We adore you O Christ and we bless you.

R. Because by your Holy Cross you have redeemed the world.

Jesus knows what He is about to embark on; He knows what He will accomplish once He ascends Calvary and is lifted above the earth on the cross. He accepts and carries the cross which becomes the sign by which we are saved.

In life, we all have many crosses that we carry. For Adele, she experienced a childhood accident and the loss of an eye. She had a meager education. And in her twenties, she had to make her home in a foreign country. Despite these crosses, Adele embraced them, submitting herself to the will of God, and living as a disciple of Jesus.

As we journey this Way of the Cross, dear Lord, please grant us the grace to accept the crosses of our lives without grumbling or complaining. Help us to know God's will through all of it.

3. Jesus Falls for the First Time

V. We adore you O Christ and we bless you.
R. Because by your Holy Cross you have redeemed the world.

Along the Way of the Cross, Jesus falls under the weight of the wood. The author of the Letter to the Hebrews reminds us that we have a High Priest who can sympathize with our weaknesses. By assuming our human nature, Jesus has redeemed our falls and sufferings.

Adele's initial response to Our Lady's mission prompted her to travel throughout the area teaching the children. At times, Adele fell underneath the pressures of distance, weather, and the negative reception from others. But when burdened by these things, she continued on, and found new ways to fulfill Our Lady's request.

As I journey this Way of the Cross, dear Lord, help me when I fall under the pressures of family and society, to pick up where I fell, and continue on my pilgrimage to the kingdom of heaven.

4. Jesus Meets His Mother, Mary

V. We adore you O Christ and we bless you.
R. Because by your Holy Cross you have redeemed the world.

Just as Mary searched for Jesus when He was lost and later found in the temple, now she searches for Him again on the streets of Jerusalem. And on the way to Calvary, their eyes meet, and a tear falls from Mary's eye. Seeing His mother gave him hopc and renewed Him as He accomplishes the purpose of His work on earth. As Mary sees her Son, she prays for Him, and those who have sentenced Him to die.

Along the way of Adele's life, she encounters the Blessed Mother, who gives her direction and a sense of mission. As the Queen of Heaven saw Adele, she saw a woman who would devote herself to labor in the Lord's vineyard. Adele sees the woman who would pray for her and send help in difficult moments.

As I journey this Way of the Cross, dear Lord, allow your mother to gaze at me with that glance of love, praying for me during my exile here below.

5. Simon of Cyrene Helps Carry the Cross

V. We adore you O Christ and we bless you.
R. Because by your Holy Cross you have redeemed the world.

The soldiers call forward Simon to help Jesus on the Way of the Cross. Jesus experiences help along that painful Way of the Cross, even if this help is for only a few moments.

When we do God's work, we all need help, especially when challenges present themselves.

Adele's family helped her promote devotion by building a small chapel; and a priest encouraged Adele to invite other women to join her work of evangelization and teaching the children.

As I journey this Way of the Cross, dear Lord, may I be inspired by the assistance of Simon of Cyrene. Reveal to me those people whom I should help. And I thank you, Lord, for those you have sent to help me throughout my life thus far.

6. Veronica Wipes the Face of Jesus

V. We adore you O Christ and we bless you.
R. Because by your Holy Cross you have redeemed the world.

Before beginning the Way of the Cross, Jesus was stripped, scourged, beaten, and crowned with thorns. His face became bloodied from the injuries He endured. Veronica steps forward from the side of the road and wipes the face of Jesus. This simple gesture becomes an act of reparation along the Way of the Cross, as Veronica wishes to console Jesus and make up for the wrong He has experienced.

When Our Lady appeared to Adele, she told us to convert and do penance. For our own sins, the sins of our family, and those of the whole world, we wish to do penance. As we make our own small acts of reparation, it is as if we wipe the face of Jesus.

As I journey this Way of the Cross, dear Lord, reveal to me opportunities to do penance, and how I can console you during my life here on earth, just like Veronica did on the way to Calvary.

7. Jesus Falls for the Second Time

V. We adore you O Christ and we bless you.
R. Because by your Holy Cross you have redeemed the world.

The help of Simon and the consoling action of Veronica assists Jesus on His ascent of the Mount; but despite these momentary helps, He grows tired and weak, and falls now a second time under the weight of the cross.

As Adele carried out her mission, she fell underneath the cross of financial hardships, forcing her to place her trust and confidence in God and the intercession of Our Lady.

As I journey this Way of the Cross, dear Lord, help me to always place my trust in your plan and surrender myself to your will for my life.

8. Jesus Meets the Women of Jerusalem

V. We adore you O Christ and we bless you.
R. Because by your Holy Cross you have redeemed the world.

Just as Jesus showed compassion to those He encountered during His years of public ministry, He continues to see the needs of others and reaches out to them. He offers consolation to the women on the streets of Jerusalem, telling them not to weep for Him, but for themselves and their children.

When Mary appeared to Adele, the Belgian settlement needed heavenly assistance. Many families had stopped practicing their faith. Today, the moral decline in our world and the lack of religious fervor causes us to mourn and weep for the people of our world. Jesus' words to the women and Mary's message remains true to this day.

As I journey this Way of the Cross, dear Lord, I pray for the world and those who do not know you. I wish to no longer weep, but to rejoice over the one repentant sinner who returns to you.

9. Jesus Falls for the Third Time

V. We adore you O Christ and we bless you.
R. Because by your Holy Cross you have redeemed the world.

In the last leg of His journey to Calvary, Jesus falls a third and final time. But He knows the purpose for which He came, and what He must do, so after a moment's rest, He picks up His cross and continues up the mountain.

When one follows God's plan for his life, there will be trials and tribulations. Adele fell under the pressure of persecution, once being asked to surrender the keys to the school and convent. God rewarded her obedience, and the bishop returned the keys to her, permitting her to continue the mission Our Lady gave her.

As I journey this Way of the Cross, dear Lord, help me to remain obedient to your will throughout my life.

10. Jesus Is Stripped of His Clothes

V. We adore you O Christ and we bless you.
R. Because by your Holy Cross you have redeemed the world.

Jesus humbled Himself by becoming like us in all things but sin. He humbled Himself by becoming obedient even to death on the cross. When Jesus is stripped of his garments, it is another act of humiliation.

All the visionaries who have seen Our Lady have endured some sort of humiliation. They are met with disbelief by family and friends. They are mocked by onlookers. Some were even arrested. The same was true for Adele, but she never faltered, believing always what Our Lady said.

As I journey this Way of the Cross, dear Lord, help me to accept humiliation out of love for you. May I never waver, but always remain faithful to You.

11. Jesus Is Nailed to the Cross

V. We adore you O Christ and we bless you.
R. Because by your Holy Cross you have redeemed the world.

Jesus reaches His final destination, where, on the altar of the cross, He would offer the sacrifice of His life. The soldiers place the nail, and with every strike, they crucify the Lord of the Universe. He writhed in pain. Blood gushed forth from His wounds. And soon, He would be suspended above the earth.

In the last years of Adele's life she experienced an accident which debilitated her. Nailed to her own cross of suffering, she offered her pain, uniting it to Jesus' suffering, for the conversion of sinners.

As I journey this Way of the Cross, dear Lord, help me to always unite my sufferings to yours for the salvation of the world.

12. Jesus Dies on the Cross

V. We adore you O Christ and we bless you.
R. Because by your Holy Cross you have redeemed the world.

Next to Jesus were two criminals, and one of them calls out for mercy, asking Jesus to remember Him when he enters into His kingdom. From the cross, Jesus prays the Psalms, and gives His final teaching by example, as He forgives His persecutors. Looking down, He saw the disciple whom He loved, John, and entrusted His mother Mary to his care. In His final action, Jesus surrenders Himself to the Father.

We stand below the cross, from which hung the Savior of the world. We stand there with Mary and John, and the others. And in death, Adele rests under the shadow of the cross, as her tombstone reads: "Sacred Cross, Under thy Shadow, I rest and hope."

As I journey this Way of the Cross, dear Lord, help me to always find solace there, that like Adele, I may now rest and hope in its shadow, which promises eternal life.

13. Jesus Is Taken Down From the Cross

V. We adore you O Christ and we bless you.
R. Because by your Holy Cross you have redeemed the world.

After the death of Jesus, the soldier pierces His side with a lance, and from that wound blood and water flowed. Once taken down from the cross, Jesus is placed in the arms of His mother, who cradles Him once again, as she did when He was an infant. She brushes His hair and kisses His face.

In death, Adele was able to see the beautiful lady, the Queen of Heaven, once again. As we journey to the kingdom of heaven, we hold on to the hope of seeing our God and meeting the angels and the saints.

As I journey this Way of the Cross, dear Lord, help me to trust in the intercession of your Blessed Mother, that at the hour of my death, she will pray for me.

14. Jesus Is Placed in the Tomb

V. We adore you O Christ and we bless you.
R. Because by your Holy Cross you have redeemed the world.

Joseph of Arimathea asks for the body of Jesus, and places Him in his own tomb. There, for three days, the lifeless body of Jesus laid, but the grave did not hold power of Jesus, for from the grave comes new life. Jesus hallowed the graves of all believers, allowing them to become a sign of hope.

Every time we visit a cemetery, it is an invitation for us to contemplate our own death and the promise of eternal life. May the Lord give eternal rest to those who have died and are buried in the little cemetery on the grounds of the National Shrine of Our Lady of Champion, and to the parents and siblings of Adele who are buried in nearby parish cemeteries.

As I journey this Way of the Cross, dear Lord, allow me not to be discouraged or lack hope at the graves of those who have died, but instead know that one day, you will call all the dead forth from the tomb into resurrected life.

Novenas to the Queen of Heaven, Our Lady of Champion

Catholics have had a longstanding tradition of praying novenas. A novena spans nine days and usually consists of specific prayers to be said each day. Many people pray novenas to Jesus, to Our Lady, or to a saint for a special intention. People will often pray novenas in anticipation of a liturgical feast (e.g., Divine Mercy Sunday, Immaculate Conception, etc.).

The novena presented here could be prayed for nine days (beginning on September 30 and ending October 8) preceding the anniversary of Our Lady's October 9 apparition. This novena may also be prayed at any time throughout the year, perhaps in anticipation of a pilgrimage to the Shrine of Our Lady of Champion or following a pilgrimage in gratitude for graces received.

This nine-day novena to Our Lady, Queen of Heaven and Our Lady of Champion has a three-fold purpose. First, to pray for Sister Adele. It is a good and noble deed to pray for the dead. Since a liturgical cult has not yet been established, we cannot formally seek Adele's intercession. Secondly, to pray for a specific daily intention which has a connection to Sister Adele or the message she received. Before each daily prayer, a reason for praying for that particular intention is given. Thirdly, to pray for your own special intention using the prayer Bishop Ricken composed to Our Lady of Champion.

A Novena to Our Lady, Queen of Heaven, and Our Lady of Champion

1. Pray the Prayer for Sister Adele
2. Pray the Daily Prayer for the day's intention
3. Pray Bishop Ricken's Prayer to Our Lady of Champion

Prayer for Sister Adele

Heavenly Father, your servant, Sister Adele, spent her life instilling in the hearts of children what they needed to know for salvation. She endured many trials and hardships because of her persistent prayer and her unending love for Jesus and Mary. We pray that in reward for her dedication to the mission entrusted to her by the Blessed Mother, you will grant her the joy of being in your presence for all eternity. Amen.

Bishop Ricken's Prayer to Our Lady of Champion

O Dear Lady of Champion, you revealed yourself as the Queen of Heaven to your servant Adele. You gave her a mission to pray for the conversion of sinners, to bring the Good News of Jesus Christ to others, and to prepare the children for the reception of the sacraments.

I trust that as you called Adele to holiness, you are calling me, in my station in life, to live a holy life, devoted to Jesus Christ with the help of your maternal love.

I bring before you now my worries and anxieties. I abandon my attachments to them and place them at your feet.

I ask you to hear the deepest longings of my heart as I pray most earnestly for ________________ (your intention).

Dear Lady, you told Adele and you say to all of us, "Do not be afraid; I will help you." Help me now as I place this intention with complete confidence and trust. Amen.

Our Father. Hail Mary. Glory Be.

Our Lady of Champion, pray for us.

Prayers for Each Day

Day One: For the Sick, Especially Those Who Suffer With Eye Disorders

Today we pray for those who are sick, especially those who suffer with eye disorders. During her childhood, Sister Adele carried the cross of being without one eye because of an accident. Moreover, Adele also had a great concern for the sick. On her death bed she told a close friend, Josie, to be kind to the sick and the old. Today we exercise that kindness by praying for them.

Dear Lady of Champion, I come to you today with complete confidence in your intercession. I bring to you all those who suffer because of illness. I pray especially for those in hospitals and nursing homes, and for those who have no one to visit them. Grant them peace in their suffering. I pray also for those who suffer from any sort of eye disorder, be it cataracts, glaucoma, or blindness. As the sick bear these crosses in their lives, I pray that they will unite their suffering to the cross of Christ for the salvation of the world.

For us too, dear Lady, please intercede. Ask the Lord to give us the grace to respond generously to those in need by our prayers, help, and support. Through your intercession, Mary, may the Lord bestow blessings upon those who work in hospitals and nursing homes as they care for the sick and the suffering, through Christ our Lord. Amen.

Day Two: For Immigrants

Today we pray for all immigrants to the United States. In 1854, Lambert and Catherine Brise decided to immigrate to the United States and settled in Red River, Wisconsin. They came seeking a better life, and it was here in the United States, in Champion, Wisconsin, where Our Lady appeared to a Belgian immigrant, their very own daughter Adele.

Dear Lady of Champion, I come to you today with complete confidence in your intercession. I bring to you all those who have had to leave their native country and seek refuge and asylum here in the United States. Some have come in order to work and send money back home to care for their families and others come with the hope of a better life. As they suffer separation from their families, grant them peace of mind. Help them to obtain all the necessities of life and proper care and treatment. Through your intercession, Mary, may the Lord bestow blessings upon these immigrants and their families, through Christ our Lord. Amen.

Day Three: For the Conversion of Sinners

Today we pray for the conversion of sinners. On October 9, 1859, Our Lady told Adele that she was the Queen of Heaven who prays for the conversion of sinners. She exhorted Adele to do the same by offering her Holy Communion for that intention. We, too, are called to this mission of prayer, prayer for ourselves and the whole world.

O Mary, you are the Queen of Heaven who prays for the conversion of sinners; please pray for me, my family, my friends, and the world. The lure of evil is all around us, consistently tempting us to sin and break God's commandments. You have appeared throughout time to remind us about your Son and His immense love and mercy. You echo the Gospel call to repentance and invite us to return to a more regular practice of the sacraments of the Church. Please pray for our world that we will return to the ways of God. Through your intercession, may sinners be granted the desire to turn away from sin and embrace the message of the Gospel.

O Mary, you are the Lady of Champion; help us, in our time of temptation, to turn toward Jesus and away from sin. This day I offer my prayer for the conversion of sinners and I make reparation for the sins I have committed and for those of the whole world. Through your intercession, Mary, may sinners be granted the desire for conversion, through Christ our Lord. Amen.

Day Four: For Parents, Catholic Schools, Religious Education Programs, and All Those Who Teach the Faith to Children as Mary requested of Adele

Today we pray for parents, Catholic schools and religious education programs, for their teachers and catechists, and for all those who teach children the faith. In addition to praying for the conversion of sinners, Our Lady told Adele to gather the children and teach them their catechism. To this end, Adele founded a Catholic school in order to fulfill this mission. She was a teacher of the Catholic faith to many young people. Let us pray today for those involved in the work of catechesis.

O Queen of Heaven, you told Adele to gather the children and teach them their catechism. I pray today for all programs of religious instruction in Catholic schools and religious education programs, especially for their teachers and catechists. Through your intercession, may those who make decisions for these institutions always keep in mind their Catholic identity. Let their goal be the promotion of Catholic teaching that is faithful to the Magisterium. Please ask your Son to grant a rich harvest of teachers and catechists who love their Catholic faith and ardently desire to share it with young people. Make them effective teachers of the Gospel. Through your intercession, Mary, may Catholic schools and religious education programs be blessed with an abundance of students, teachers, and catechists, and may parents, as first educators, teach their children well, through Christ our Lord. Amen.

Day Five: For Students

Gathering the children was the instruction given to Adele by Our Lady. Today we pray for students, that they may be open to the gift of faith.

O Lady of Champion, today I entrust to your intercession all students of Catholic schools and religious education programs and homeschools. Please ask Jesus to open their hearts to the teachings of the Church. Please wrap your mantle of protection around our young people. Keep them safe from the danger of sin and the enticement of evil. Help them to fall deeper in love with Jesus and the Church. Through your intercession, Mary, may young people be granted the desire to follow Jesus in their daily lives, through Christ our Lord. Amen.

Day 6: For Families

Today we pray for families. Adele was blessed to have the support of her parents after the apparition. Her father helped to build the first chapels commemorating Our Lady's apparitions. Let us pray for holy families.

O Lady of Champion, today I bring to you the families of the world. Today there are so many broken families. Divorce is rampant, husbands and wives are unfaithful to each other, single parenthood is on the rise, and there are fatherless homes, among so many other problems. The family is under attack. Please intercede especially for any families I know that are going through a difficult time. Help them to overcome their difficult situation. O Mary, please pray for the sanctification of families. May family prayer once again be a part of each household. Through your intercession, Mary, may there be many holy families and from those families, vocations to the priesthood and consecrated life, through Christ our Lord. Amen.

Day 7: For Priests

Today we pray for priests. Through Adele's life, she worked closely with priests. It was under the guidance of Fr. Verhoef that Adele founded a tertiary group of Franciscan sisters. After Adele had prepared individuals for the sacraments of confession and Eucharist, she presented them to a priest for admission to the sacraments. When confronted by the bishop, she obediently followed his directive. Whenever she encountered a perplexing situation, be it her immigration to the United States or the mysterious woman she had seen twice, she sought out the guidance of the local priest.

O Lady of Champion, today I bring to your intercession all priests and bishops. It was by your *fiat*, your yes, that we were given our eternal priest, Jesus Christ. We pray for our priests, that they will conform their lives to the will of God through obedience to their bishop and the Magisterium. May they be men of prayer who are dedicated to serving the Lord and the people entrusted to their care. In times of loneliness and doubt, grant them comfort and peace in knowing that they are doing God's will. Through your intercession, Mary, may all priests be granted the grace of a missionary heart and zeal for souls, through Christ our Lord. Amen.

Day 8: For the Return of Those Away From the Sacraments and for a Renewed Religious Fervor

Today we pray for the return of those away from the sacramental life of the Church and for a renewed religious fervor among the Catholic faithful. Adele was instructed to make a general confession and offer her communion for the conversion of sinners. She was called to participate in the sacramental life of the Church and to bring others to the sacraments through catechesis. Adele was also told to gather the children and teach them how to approach the sacraments.

O Lady of Champion, today I entrust to your intercession those who are away from the practice of their Catholic faith and for a renewal of religious fervor among all Catholics. Throughout all your many appearances, you have always directed your children to the sacraments. Often at these holy sites, people return to the sacrament of Penance, perhaps after being away for many years. There is a spiritual hunger in our world that can only be satiated by Christ, the sacraments, and the Word of God.

O Mary, please touch the hearts of all those who have fallen away from the sacraments; grant them the desire for confession so that they can worthily receive your Son again in the Eucharist. O Mary, please pray also for a renewed religious fervor among the Catholic faithful. May we never take the sacraments for granted, especially the Eucharist, and may we always receive your Son worthily in Holy Communion. Please accept my prayers as reparation for those who receive the Eucharist in a state of mortal sin. Through your intercession, Mary, may God's holy people realize again the treasure of the sacraments of the Church, through Christ our Lord. Amen.

Day 9: For the New Evangelization

Today we pray for the New Evangelization that the popes of the modern era have initiated. In the Gospel of

Matthew, before His ascension, Jesus instructed the disciples to "Go forth and make disciples of all nations, baptizing them in the name of the Father, and of the Son, and of the Holy Spirit." This is the call to spread the faith and evangelize our world. Juan Diego's faith led to the evangelization and conversion of an entire country, Adele Brise evangelized the area around the Door Peninsula, and today we are called to bear witness to the Gospel message of Jesus Christ to those around us.

O Queen of Heaven, you appeared in the New World to Juan Diego and gave him the *tilma*—upon which we see your image. Through this miraculous image, millions of Native Americans converted to the Catholic faith. To Adele Brise, you gave a blueprint for catechesis; gather the children in this wild country and teach them what they need to know for salvation, their catechism, how to sign themselves with the Sign of the Cross, and how to approach the sacraments.

O Mary, you have been hailed as the Star of the New Evangelization. Guide the Church as she embarks on this mission of spreading the Gospel. May the Lord bless the Church's laborers and those to whom she ministers. Grant to them, through your intercession, receptivity to the message of

Christ. Open their hearts and their minds to the Gospel. O Mary, Star of the New Evangelization, please pray for the Church, and through your intercession may many more members be added to her flock, through Christ our Lord. Amen.

Mary Help Us! A Novena of Mary's Helping Titles

Mary has appeared throughout the centuries to renew the faith of a particular time and region. The messages she spoke seem to transcend time and remain relevant to our present experience of the Church in the third millennium. She has graced us with her presence at Tepeyac Hill (Guadalupe), Rue du Bac (Miraculous Medal), La Salette, Lourdes, Fatima, Beauraing, and Banneux, to name just a few. In the United States, in October of 1859, one year after the apparitions received in Lourdes, France by St. Bernadette Soubirous, the Mother of God chose to reveal herself to a humble, simple, twenty-eight-year-old Belgian immigrant named Adele Brise. Adele's life changed after her third encounter with the Blessed Virgin because she received from her a mission of prayer and catechesis, to which Adele dedicated the rest of her life.

Today, the National Shrine of Our Lady of Champion in Champion, Wisconsin, commemorates the 1859 apparitions of the Queen of Heaven received by Brise. For over 150 years, Catholics and Christians alike made pilgrimages to this sacred place where Mary appeared. They prayed for healing and entrusted their petitions to the Queen of Heaven, venerated also under the title Our Lady of Champion. These pilgrims came out of faith, even though the Church had not officially approved the apparitions. That is, until December 8, 2010, when in a historic decree, Bishop David Ricken formally approved the apparitions as worthy of belief, although not obligatory among the Christian faithful, making the Wisconsin apparition the first and only approved Marian apparition in the United States. Overnight, an unknown apparition of the Blessed Virgin was catapulted into the national and international spotlight, and to this day the shrine commemorating the apparitions has never been the same.

This novena draws upon nine different titles of Mary, which emphasize the "Good Help" we wish to ask Mary to obtain for us and for special intentions related to the message Mary spoke as well as the life of Sister Adele. The novena is prayed in the following way, beginning with the **Daily Prayer**, followed by **Bishop Ricken's prayer to Our Lady of Champion**, and ***optionally***, a person may wish to pray the **Litany to Our Lady of Champion**.

Through the intercession of Mary, the Queen of Heaven and Our Lady of Champion, may you place great trust and confidence in her intercession, and by God's grace, may you return to the National Shrine or make your pilgrimage in order to give thanks for the graces obtained during this novena.

Day 1: Queen of Heaven

Today we ask the intercession of Mary under the title Queen of Heaven. When Adele asked her heavenly visitor who she was, the woman answered: "I am the Queen of Heaven who prays for the conversion of sinners."

Queen of Heaven, we thank your son, the King, for sending you to us and blessing us with your presence and message. Today, we join you in praying for the conversion of sinners. Show us your good help and obtain from your son the conversion of our family members, friends, and the entire world. May your prayers, on our behalf, help all believers to follow the commands of the Lord and to walk in His paths.

See the appendix for Bishop Ricken's prayer to Our Lady of Champion and the Litany to Our Lady of Champion.

Day 2: Mother of Mercy

Today we ask the intercession of Mary under the title Mother of Mercy. Mary commended Adele for her reception of the Eucharist and encouraged her to make a general confession. Today many pilgrims to the shrine seek God's mercy through the sacrament of Reconciliation.

Mother of Mercy, we thank your son Jesus for shedding His blood on the cross and redeeming us from our sins. Today, we implore your intercession for those who have sought conversion in their lives. They are the answer to your prayers and ours. To your motherly intercession, we entrust pilgrims' past, present, and future. As they experience God's mercy at the National Shrine of Our

Lady of Champion and in their local communities, may the grace of the sacrament strengthen them in turning away from sin and remaining faithful to God. Show your good help to those who seek your Son's mercy and forgiveness and obtain for them a firm purpose of amendment.

Day 3: Health of the Sick

Today we ask the intercession of Mary under the title Health of the Sick. At the end of Adele's life, she told her friend Josie, "Be kind to the sick and the old, and continue to instruct the old in their religion." On account of Adele's passion for the sick, the shrine today has become a place of prayer for healing for many pilgrims.

Mary, Health of the Sick, we thank your son Jesus for the healing graces pilgrims have received at the National Shrine of Our Lady of Champion. To your motherly intercession, we entrust pilgrims' past, present, and future as they seek healing in mind, body, and spirit. Show your good help to those who are sick and obtain for them healing, comfort, and consolation from your son, Jesus.

Day 4: Queen of Families

Today we ask the intercession of Mary under the title Queen of Families. Adele shared the news of the apparition with her family. Her father helped to construct the first chapel commemorating the apparition. Adele faithfully carried out her apostolate in those initial years following the apparition and entered the homes of many families to teach their children.

Queen of Families, we thank your son Jesus for the family of Sister Adele and for all families who have visited the Shrine of Our Lady of Champion. To your motherly intercession, we entrust all the families of the world: faithful families, faithless families, and broken families. Gather all families under your mantle of love and protection. Show to them your good help, and from your Son obtain for them an increase of faith, hope, and love, and the graces of unity, healing, perseverance, and whatever else they may need.

Day 5: Mother of Disciples

Today we ask the intercession of Mary under the title Mother of Disciples. The Queen of Heaven exhorted Adele to gather the children and teach them their catechism.

Let us pray in a special way for catechists, that as they live their lives of discipleship, they may lead others to become disciples.

Mother of Disciples, we thank your son Jesus for inviting us to become His disciples, and to your motherly intercession we entrust all catechists charged with the responsibility of forming disciples. Through the message you spoke to Adele, you invited her to a life of discipleship with your Son, and as we carry on her mission, the same is true for us. Through your motherly assistance, help all Christians become faith filled disciples and followers of Jesus. Show us your good help and obtain for us the grace to always sit at the feet of your Son and learn from Him.

Day 6: Our Lady of Vocations

Today we ask the intercession of Mary under the title Our Lady of Vocations. Adele discerned the events of her life with various priests and she was obedient to the bishop's request. Several years after the apparition, Adele became known as Sister Adele, after she founded a tertiary group of Franciscan sisters.

Our Lady of Vocations, we thank your son Jesus for calling all people to follow you in their vocational path, and for the many priests you placed in the life of Sister Adele, helping her to respond to your will for her life. We give thanks also for the gift of consecrated religious who serve the Lord, and for the prompting and guidance of Adele to found a third-order of Franciscan sisters to fulfill Our Lady's mission for her. To your motherly intercession, we entrust our priests and consecrated religious and we ask you to help our priests as they lead your faithful and offer spiritual counsel and our consecrated religious in the work your son Jesus has called them to do. Show your good help to the Church's priests and consecrated religious and obtain for them the graces they need to live their vocations faithfully and with great joy and love.

Day 7: Queen of Peace

Today we ask the intercession of Mary under the title Queen of Peace. Mary appeared in 1859 to Adele, a few years before the Civil War in the United States. In her apparition, Mary told Adele she prayed for the conversion of sinners and wanted her to do the same. Peace can only happen when hearts begin to change.

Queen of Peace, we thank your son Jesus for the gift of peace which He has left us. We entrust to your motherly intercession our world and its desperate need for peace. Change the hearts of those who seek to foster violence and division. Wrap your mantle of protection around those who serve in the military and armed forces. Bring them safely home and offer the gift of comfort to their families. Show us your good help and obtain for us from your Son an end to terrorism, war, and violence.

Day 8: Star of the New Evangelization

Today we ask the intercession of Mary under the title Star of the New Evangelization. Recent popes hailed Mary under this title as the Church undertakes the task of evangelizing a new generation of Catholics. The 2010 approval of the Wisconsin apparition places Mary's 1859 message at the heart of the new evangelization.

Mary, Star of the New Evangelization, we thank your son Jesus for allowing us to live in this age of the Church and for the task He has entrusted to us. The mission you entrusted to Adele is a star which guides us to the sacraments and catechesis. Our time is just like Adele's, which was marked by a lax practice of faith. She needed your message then and we need your message now. Show to us, your devoted servants, your good help and obtain for the Church a renewal in belief and practice of the faith.

Day 9: Our Lady of Good Help

Today we ask the intercession of Mary under the title Our Lady of Good Help. Adele Brise insisted on dedicating the chapels commemorating the apparition under this title. The devotion to Notre Dame de Bon Secours, which is centuries old, can be traced to France, Belgium, and Canada. In the province of Belgium where Adele grew up, the devotion was widespread.

Our Lady of Good Help, we thank your son Jesus for the ways He has allowed you to serve as our advocate and intercessor, and for the graces you have obtained for us through this novena. As a mother, you wish to help all your children in their need as they cry out to you. Help those who are sick, homeless, and poor. Help the immigrants and refugees. Help families, priests, consecrated religious, and those who live in the single state. Help the Church in her work of catechesis and evangelization. O Queen of Heaven, do not despise the petitions we have offered, but show us your good help and obtain from your Son what is in accord with His holy and wonderful providence.

Praying With Our Lady's Message to Adele

Forty days after the Resurrection, Jesus climbed the Mount of Olives and gave His final exhortation before ascending into heaven in the sight of His apostles, and traditionally depicted in iconography, the Blessed Virgin Mary. In the nine days that followed, the apostles and the Blessed Mother gathered in the Upper Room, united in prayer for the coming of the promised Holy Spirit (See Acts 1:14). On the fiftieth day, Pentecost, tongues of fire descended upon them. This was the first **novena** or nine days of prayer in the Church.

Catholics throughout the world pray novenas as a form of devotional prayer, especially when an urgent need arises. Their days of prayer might be directed to the Divine Mercy, a popular novena beginning on Good Friday and ending on Divine Mercy Sunday (the First Sunday after Easter). It was Jesus himself who requested the novena in a series of apparitions received by a Polish sister named St. Faustina Kowalska. Others turn to Mary or the saints, hoping they will intercede on their behalf before the throne of God.

Today, Catholics from around the world visit the National Shrine of Our Lady of Champion and pray to receive special graces. They sense the maternal presence of Mary and receive comfort from her prayers. This novena's prayers present fragments of Mary's message to Adele each day allowing us an opportunity to pray with Mary's words and interiorize the message Mary spoke. The national novena begins on October 1 and ends October 9, the anniversary of Mary's message, but this novena could be prayed anytime of the year. Each day there are two prayers: the Daily Novena Prayer and the Prayer to Our Lady of Champion composed by Bishop David Ricken which provides the opportunity for you to pray for whatever your intentions might be. Please prayerfully join Catholics from the Diocese of Green Bay and throughout the world, in addition to the pilgrims who will visit the National Shrine of Our Lady of Champion, in praying this novena. Let us listen to Mary's words, pray with them, and live them every day of our lives.

Day One: Queen of Heaven

"I Am the Queen of Heaven."

O Mary, you were chosen to be the mother of the Savior, and reign now as the Queen Mother. We salute you as the Queen of Heaven, knowing that you are our intercessor and advocate. You are the Queen of Heaven and Earth, the Queen of Peace, the Queen of Apostles, and the Queen of Clergy. I ask you today to be the Queen of my heart, my family, my diocese, and my country.

Day Two: Renewal of Sacramental Life

"You received Holy Communion this morning, and that is well. But you must do more. Make a general confession."

O Mary, you are the mother of the Church, and always direct us to the source of God's love found in the sacraments. Please intercede for our Church today. Renew among the faithful a belief in Christ's true presence in the Eucharist. Through your motherly intercession, draw the faithful back to the sacrament of Reconciliation so they may know your Son's love for them. As our mother, please keep inviting us to return to your Son and accompanying us on our pilgrimage to the kingdom of heaven.

Day Three: Conversion of Sinners

"Offer your Holy Communion for the conversion of sinners."

O Mary, you told Adele you were the Queen of Heaven who prays for the conversion of sinners. Just as you invited Adele to unite with you in that prayer, I wish to do the same today. I join you in praying for me, the unworthy sinner that I am, but also for my family, friends, coworkers, country, and the entire world. As we listen to the words of your son in the Gospel, may your intercession gain for us a conversion of heart, and repentance for our sins, so one day we may inherit the kingdom of heaven.

Day Four: Workers in the Vineyard

"Why are you standing here in idleness while your companions are working in the vineyard of my Son?"

O Mary, you were one of the first to spread the good news as you carried the Christ child in your womb to visit your cousin Elizabeth. Today, your Son calls each of us to service in His vineyard, just as He called Adele long ago. Help us, in whatever vocation we live, to never be idle, but always ready to proclaim the good news to whomever we meet. In a special way, I ask you to intercede and obtain from your Son many graces for those who serve as missionaries, priests, and consecrated religious.

Day Five: For Believers and Unbelievers

"Blessed are those who believe without seeing."

O Mary, you commended the faith of Adele's companions who knelt at her command. Look with love upon those who visit the National Shrine of Our Lady of Champion in faith that you will intercede for their intentions. May the stories of those who have received graces from this Shrine touch the hearts of those who do not believe. Open the eyes of all to the wonders that are around them, and through your intercession, obtain for them the grace of belief.

Day Six: Reparation

"Convert and do penance."

O Mary, you have asked in many apparitions for us to do penance and make reparation for sin which offends God. Help us by your prayers so we may know the areas of our lives in which we need conversion and enlighten our minds to know the sins of our past for which we need to repent. I pray that the sacrifices and penance I make may be found pleasing to you, my mother, and to Almighty God.

Day Seven: For Youth

"Gather the children."

O Mary, with a mother's love you want all to know about your Son and God's love for them, young and old alike. As you instructed Adele to gather the children and teach them, we ask you to pray for all our young people. By your intercession, obtain for them an open mind and heart so they may desire a deeper relationship with God and live according to his commands.

Day Eight: For Teachers and Catechists

"Teach them what they should know for salvation."

O Mary, your Son endows His servants with many gifts, and calls individuals to serve Him in different ways. As our mother, look with love upon all those who dedicate themselves to teaching young people as teachers or catechists. Intercede before the throne of God for them, so they may be effective communicators of the gospel. May their love for God and the Church serve as a witness to all they meet.

Day Nine: For all our needs

"Go and fear nothing, I will help you."

O Mary, you are our mother and intercessor. To you do we cry, as the poor banished children of Eve, to you do we send up our sighs, mourning, and weeping in this valley of tears. You told Adele to fear nothing, echoing the words you heard at the Annunciation. I trust these words are meant for me. As I place my confidence in your intercession, I surrender all my fears and worries of life to Jesus through your immaculate hands. Fulfill your promise of help, and obtain from your Son whatever graces He wishes to impart to me while I make my pilgrimage on earth to the heavenly kingdom.

A Novena for the Conversion of Sinners

The very first words Mary spoke to Adele Brise on October 9, 1859 revolved around conversion. Mary identified herself as the Queen of Heaven who prays for the conversion of sinners. She went on to encourage Adele to offer her Holy Communion for that intention. According to author Susan Tassone, the number one prayer request worldwide voiced to clergy, on radio and television network shows, and to Catholic organizations is for conversion. It's a petition that's personal and hits close to home for many. Parents are concerned for their children who no longer practice the faith. Looking around at everything going on in the world reminds us to pray for the conversion of those who find themselves at odds with God, the Church, and moral teachings.

During this novena, we unite our prayers to the Queen of Heaven who prays for the conversion of sinners. We pray with her and strive to fulfill her request; namely, that we also pray for the conversion of sinners. Throughout Sister Adele's life, she surely prayed for the conversion of many people. That conversion began with herself, as she went to the sacrament of Reconciliation and asked forgiveness for her sins. I'm sure she prayed for the children she taught and their families. During her life, she encountered individuals who exhibited immoral behavior, at times, possibly costing Adele her mission and hurting her reputation. Then there was Joseph Rene Vilatte, the priest of the Old Catholic Church, a heretical sect, who sought to convert Catholics to his belief. The work of Vilatte troubled Adele, and she likely entrusted him to Mary's intercession. At the end of Vilatte's life, he was reconciled to the Church and took up a life of penance.

Mary's invitation to pray for conversion is perhaps one of the most overlooked aspects of her message. In this novena, we strive to honor Our Lady's request, and ask for the grace of conversion for those we love, and for sinners throughout the Church and the world. Each day there is a general intention for conversion, but you may wish to pray the novena each day for someone you know and love. During this novena, it might be efficacious to attend Mass as often as you are able and to offer your Holy Communion for the conversion of sinners, just as Adele did and Mary requested.

Day One: For Myself

Dear Queen of Heaven, I join you in praying for the conversion of sinners. Please pray for me, as I strive daily to convert my life. Obtain for me the grace to know my sins, to confess them, and never to commit them again. Please pray for me, dear mother, that I might have patience with myself as I try to convert my life, patience with others who I am praying for in this novena, and patience and trust in God, that He will utilize my prayers during these nine days, as I unite them to those of the Blessed Mother, desiring for her prayers for the conversion of sinners to be answered. Dear Lord, hear the prayers of your mother, and grant me the grace of conversion. Amen.

Day Two: For My Family and Friends

Dear Queen of Heaven, I join you in praying for the conversion of sinners. Today, I pray for my family and friends. At times my soul is troubled by the things they do or fail to do. Obtain for them the grace to know the areas of life where Jesus is inviting them to conversion and change. For those who do not love God with their whole heart; for those who do not attend Mass each week; for those who take God's name in vain; for those who struggle with addictions; for those engaged in a lifestyle of sin, please pray for them so that they might know God's love and strive to follow Him every day of their lives so that one day they may live with Him forever in heaven. Dear Lord, hear the prayers of your mother, and grant my family and friends the grace of conversion. Amen.

Day Three: For the Culture

Dear Queen of Heaven, I join you in praying for the conversion of sinners. Today I ask you to pray for our society and culture, especially for an end to the immorality that surrounds us. Mother Mary, pray for those contemplating abortion, for couples who contracept, for those struggling with pornography, and for those contemplating physician-assisted suicide. Pray for an end to racism, hatred, and all other ungodliness in our society. We ask your prayers, dear Lady, that all of humanity will regain an appreciation for the image and likeness of God imprinted upon every human person. Obtain for us many graces, so that our hearts might turn toward God and peace might reign in our hearts and land. Dear Lord, hear the prayers of your mother, and grant our culture the grace of conversion. Amen.

Day Four: For Governments

Dear Queen of Heaven, I join you in praying for the conversion of sinners. Today I ask you to pray for the governments of the world. Mother Mary, pray for those elected to public office; turn their hearts from declaring war to fostering peace; from disregarding the value of human life to the recognizing the inherent dignity of all life; from ignoring the plight of the poor to a great concern for those in need. Please pray for all government leaders, that they may always regard the authority of Christ and Divine Law as supreme in their land so that Christ's peace might reign over all things. Dear Lord, hear the prayers of your mother, and grant our political, civil, and military authorities the grace of conversion. Amen.

Day Five: For the Clergy and Consecrated Religious

Dear Queen of Heaven, I join you in praying for the conversion of sinners. Today I ask you to pray for the clergy and consecrated religious. Those who serve God are not immune from committing sin, and some have grievously sinned against our children. Mother Mary, please pray for them, that they may be protected from the lure of the evil one; safeguard them against temptation, and give them true conversion of heart so that they may love God and His holy people with the love of Jesus' Sacred Heart. I pray also for those who promote false teaching; obtain for them the grace of conversion to know the Truth as it has been revealed by Christ and taught by His holy Church. Dear Lord, hear the prayers of your mother, and grant our priests and consecrated religious the grace of conversion. Amen.

Day Six: For Young People

Dear Queen of Heaven, I join you in praying for the conversion of sinners. Today I ask you to pray for the young people of our world. Mother Mary, please pray for them, and protect them from the contagion of the world which fosters discord and hate. Convert their hearts, so there will be no more violence. Protect them from immoral lifestyles and impurity. Convict their hearts with the Truth of Christ's teaching, the Gospel, and the morality taught by the Catholic Church. Obtain for them from your Son a hunger for knowledge and a love of God and neighbor. Dear Lord, hear the prayers of your mother, and grant young people the grace of conversion. Amen.

Day Seven: For Fallen Away Catholics

Dear Queen of Heaven, I join you in praying for the conversion of sinners. Today I ask you to pray for those who have fallen way from the practice of their faith. I am reminded that this is one of the reasons you must have appeared to Adele, to renew the faith of the Belgian immigrants. Mother Mary, please pray for those who no longer find nourishment in the Eucharist. As I unite my prayers to yours for them, may they serve as a divine spark, welling up within their souls a desire for the Eucharist. Mother Mary, please pray also for those who are away from the sacrament of Reconciliation. May our prayers begin the process of their response to Christ's invitation to receive His mercy. O Queen of Heaven, obtain from your Son the grace of converted souls and churches filled with disciples of Jesus. Dear Lord, hear the prayers of your mother, and grant fallen away Catholics the grace of conversion. Amen.

Day Eight: Those Who Do Not Believe in God

Dear Queen of Heaven, I join you in praying for the conversion of sinners. Today I ask you to pray for those who do not believe in God. Some believe without seeing, like the companions of Adele, whom you commended for their belief. Mother Mary, please pray for all who do not yet believe and know God as Father, Son, and Holy Spirit. May they soon approach the font of Baptism, in the fullness of their conversion of life. Obtain for them this grace. Dear Lord, hear the prayers of your mother, and grant those who do not believe in God the grace of conversion. Amen.

Day Nine: For Our Enemies

Dear Queen of Heaven, I join you in praying for the conversion of sinners. Today I ask you to pray for my enemies and for the enemies of the Church. I pray for those who misunderstand who I am and what I believe; for those who are offended by my beliefs and those of the Church. By your prayers, mother Mary, may the things that divide us be conquered, and may all know the Truth of your Divine Son. Dear Lord, hear the prayers of your mother, and grant to my enemies, and the enemies of the Church, the grace of conversion. Amen.

A Novena for Healing

Healing is often one of the graces associated with Marian intercession, places of devotion, and apparition sites. Over the past century and a half, pilgrims have asked Mary's prayers for the healing of many infirmities. Healings of all kinds occur at the National Shrine of Our Lady of Champion and other religious shrines throughout the world.

Adele told her friend Josie to be kind to the old and the sick and to continue to instruct the youth in their religion as she had done. Adele had a special concern for the sick. During her lifetime, she witnessed medical epidemics plague her community, and at one point in the shrine's history, it became a home for crippled children. As a shrine dedicated to the Blessed Mother and a site of Marian apparition, the National Shrine of Our Lady of Champion attracts pilgrims of various backgrounds. Many of them come seeking Mary's prayers for a special intention, oftentimes for their healing or that of a loved one.

This novena presents to devotees a variety of healing prayers and intentions over the span of nine days. It can be prayed in anticipation of a pilgrimage to the shrine, begun on the day of your pilgrimage and extending your prayer for nine days afterward, or from your home as you pray for those in need of healing mercies and graces.

Day One: For My Own Healing

Dear Lady of Champion, you offer the help of your prayers to those who call upon your intercession. At the wedding feast in Cana, you noticed the needs of the couple before anyone else, and you sought to help them in their hour of need. From your place in heaven, you see my needs, and know the areas of healing I need in my life, healing that I might not even know I need. Please pray for me, that the Lord will grant to me healing of any illness I might have, healing of my mind, and healing of my soul. Dear Jesus, you are the Divine Physician; please hear my prayers, and those of your mother, and grant me the grace of healing. Amen.

Day Two: For the Healing of My Family

Dear Lady of Champion, you offer the help of your prayers to those who call upon your intercession. At the wedding feast in Cana, you noticed the needs of the couple before anyone else, and you sought to help them in their hour of need. From your place in heaven, you see the needs of my family, and know the healing they need. Please pray for them, that the Lord will grant healing to those of my family who are sick and healing to those who struggle with addictions. Obtain for them healing of mind and soul too. May your prayers gain for us the healing of any hurt or division so that we all might be reconciled and extend forgiveness to one another. Dear Jesus, you are the Divine Physician; please hear my prayers, and those of your mother, and grant to my family the grace of healing. Amen.

Day Three: For My Friends Who Need Healing

Dear Lady of Champion, you offer the help of your prayers to those who call upon your intercession. At the wedding feast in Cana, you noticed the needs of the couple before anyone else, and you sought to help them in their hour of need. From your place in heaven, you see the needs of my friends, and know the healing they need. Please pray for them, that the Lord will grant healing to those of my friends who are sick, healing to those who struggle with addictions. Obtain for them healing of mind and soul. For any hurt I have caused, help us to forgive each other so that our friendship may be healed and strengthened. Dear Jesus, you are the Divine Physician; please hear my prayers, and those of your mother, and grant to my friends the grace of healing. Amen.

Day Four: For the Blind and Deaf

Dear Lady of Champion, you offer the help of your prayers to those who call upon your intercession. At the wedding feast in Cana, you noticed the needs of the couple before anyone else, and you sought to help them in their hour of need. Please pray for those who are blind and deaf. Your Son, Jesus, opened the eyes of the blind and the ears of the deaf. Obtain for them the grace to see the wonders of the world and to hear the sounds of creation. Dear Jesus, you are the Divine Physician; please hear my prayers, and those of your mother, and grant to the blind and deaf the grace of healing. Amen.

Day Five: For Those Fighting Cancer

Dear Lady of Champion, you offer the help of your prayers to those who call upon your intercession. At the wedding feast in Cana, you noticed the needs of the couple before anyone else, and you sought to help them in their hour of need. Please see now the needs of those with cancer and pray for them. Petition your Son for a complete healing of (name person). Help them as they continue to fight. Strengthen them against the side effects of chemotherapy, radiation, and other forms of treatment. Mother Mary, pray for their families, who feel helpless as they watch their loved one fight. I pray also for medical researchers; help them to soon find a cure. I entrust my family and friends who have died of cancer to your maternal intercession; pray for them, that if detained in purgatory, they soon will behold God face to face. And please, fulfill your promise, dear Mother, should those struggling with cancer not be healed, please be with them at the hour of their death. Dear Jesus, you are the Divine Physician; please hear my prayers, and those of your mother, and grant to those fighting cancer the grace of healing. Amen.

Day Six: For Those With any Illness

Dear Lady of Champion, you offer the help of your prayers to those who call upon your intercession. At the wedding feast in Cana, you noticed the needs of the couple before anyone else, and you sought to help them in their hour of need. Please see now the needs of those who struggle with any type of illness. Ask your Son to grant them a full healing of their illness. If such a request is not according to God's providence, stand beside them in their suffering, just as you stood beneath the cross of your Son. Obtain for them relief of their symptoms and peace of mind. Intercede for their doctors and caregivers as they provide care and treatment. Dear Jesus, you are the Divine Physician; please hear my prayers, and those of your mother, and grant to those who are sick the grace of healing. Amen.

Day Seven: For the Healing of My Memory

Dear Lady of Champion, you offer the help of your prayers to those who call upon your intercession. At the wedding feast in Cana, you noticed the needs of the couple before anyone else, and you sought to help them in their hour of need. Please pray for the healing of my memory. I know that there are things I have watched or seen that still reside in my mind, and at times bring me discomfort and anxiety. I desire to forget all the harsh words people have said to me or about me. I surrender them all into the merciful hands of Jesus. Help me to remember all that is good, and that Jesus has redeemed me by His death on the cross. Dear Jesus, you are the Divine Physician; please hear my prayers, and those of your mother, and grant me the grace of healing, especially in my memory. Amen.

Day Eight: For the Healing of My Wounds

Dear Lady of Champion, you offer the help of your prayers to those who call upon your intercession. At the wedding feast in Cana, you noticed the needs of the couple before anyone else, and you sought to help them in their hour of need. Please pray for the healing of my wounds. I know that different people, events, and experiences have caused doubts to rise up within my heart, mind, and soul. Obtain for me healing from the wounds of abandonment, distrust, and of not being loved. Pray for me, that I might be delivered from the fears of rejection and healed from any abuse that I have endured. Mother Mary, may your example of forgiving those who crucified your Son help me to forgive those who have wounded me. I wish to be healed and submit everything from my past to the healing mercy of Christ. Dear Jesus, Divine Physician, please hear my prayers, and those of your mother, and grant me the grace of healing, especially of all my wounds. Amen.

Day Nine: For the Healing of Those I Have Injured

Dear Lady of Champion, you offer the help of your prayers to those who call upon your intercession. At the wedding feast in Cana, you noticed the needs of the couple before anyone else, and you sought to help them in their hour of need. Please pray for the healing of those who I have injured by my words or actions. By my own sinfulness, I have hurt others in the things that I have said to them or about them to others and by the things that I have done or failed to do. To those who struggle mentally, psychologically, or emotionally on account of me, please dear mother, obtain from your Son whatever healing they need. By your example, inspire them to be able to forgive me, and petition your Son that I might be able to forgive myself. Dear Jesus, Divine Physician, please hear my prayers and those of your mother, and grant the grace of healing to those whom I have injured. Amen.

Additional Prayers and Litanies

The following prayers were inspired by the life of Adele, the message Mary spoke, and devotion to Mary promoted at the Shrine.

Prayer After Communion for the Conversion of Sinners

Eternal Father, I kneel before you this day with a grateful heart because you have allowed me to receive the body and blood of your son Jesus in Holy Communion.

Thank you for sending the Queen of Heaven to earth with a message calling us to conversion and emphasizing the sacraments. For when she appeared to Adele Brise in 1859, she asked her to offer her Holy Communion for the conversion of sinners. Just as Adele did long ago, I wish to do likewise this day.

I offer to you, Eternal Father, the body, blood, soul, and divinity of your Son for the conversion of sinners, including myself, in reparation for sin, and the salvation of souls and *(pause to name specific individual/group).*

Through Our Lady's maternal solicitude, may the hearts of hardened sinners return to the sacraments of Penance and Eucharist, especially to Sunday Mass and to daily prayer. As I go forward from this holy Mass, help me to fear nothing, knowing that you are with me and are always guiding me, and that Our Lady constantly intercedes for me. Make me aware of your presence this day and always. Amen.

Litany of Our Lady of Champion, the Lady of Good Help

V. Lord, have mercy. R. Lord have mercy.
V. Christ, have mercy. R. Christ have mercy.
V. Lord, have mercy. R. Christ have mercy.
V. Christ, hear us.
R. Christ, graciously hear us.
God the Father of Heaven, have mercy on us.
God the Son, Redeemer of the world, have mercy on us.

God the Holy Spirit, have mercy on us.
Holy Trinity, one God, have mercy on us.

Response: Pray for Us

Holy Mary,
Holy Mother of God,
Queen of Heaven,
Star of the Sea,
Comforter of the Afflicted,
Health of the Sick,
Refuge of Sinners,
Star of the New Evangelization,
Our Lady of Good Help,

Response: Mary Help Us

In times of temptation,
In times of sickness,
In times of sorrow,
In times of confusion,
In times of persecution,
In times of failure,
In times of betrayal,
In times of weakness,
In times of discernment,
In times of war,

Response: Mary Help Them

For those who are unemployed,
For those who are homeless,
For those who struggle to make ends meet,
For those in troubled marriages,
For those contemplating abortion,
For those contemplating suicide,
For those who are sick,
For those suffering with physical handicaps,
For those unable to conceive,
For those trapped in a life of sin,
For those who suffer from addictions,
For those near death,
For those who do not believe in God,
For those who have rejected God's commandments,
For fallen away Catholics,
For those who need our prayers,
For the immigrant,
For the poor souls in purgatory,
For teachers and catechists,
For Catholic schools and universities,
For Catholic parishes,
For bishops, priests, deacons, and seminarians,
For consecrated religious,

For missionaries,
For families,

V. Lamb of God, who takes away the sins of the world,
R. Spare us, O Lord.
V. Lamb of God, who takes away the sins of the world,
R. Graciously hear us, O Lord.
V. Lamb of God, who takes away the sins of the world,
R. Have mercy on us.

V. Pray for us, O holy Mother of God.
R. That we may be made worthy of the promises of Christ.

Let us pray, Grant O God, through the intercession and mediation of Our Lady of Good Help and Our Lady of Champion, all the graces we need to live a life in accordance with your will. Come to the help of your servants who are in need of heavenly assistance. Incline your ear to the prayers offered by them through the intercession of the Queen of Heaven, through Christ our Lord. Amen.

Consecration to Jesus Through Our Lady, Queen of Heaven, Our Lady of Champion

O Mother Mary, Queen of Heaven, Our Lady of Champion, I come to you this day, just as I am, knowing that I am a sinner. Yet I place my confidence in the infinite mercy and love of God. O Dear Lady, you asked for the conversion of sinners, instructed Adele to teach the young children, and entrusted to her this great mission of prayer and evangelization.

I give my life to Jesus through your hands, so that everything I am, everything I do, and everything I say may be for the greater honor and glory of your Son. Through your intercession, may your Son use me and dispose of me in whatever way He wishes for the salvation of souls. Help me to love every person I meet with the heart of Jesus, by imitating your virtues and those of your Son. I consecrate to you my entire life, so that I can be enveloped within the mission to which you have called us: a mission of prayer and catechesis for the salvation of souls.

This day I desire to be counted among the number of your children, who in a special way have given themselves entirely to you, and through you, to Jesus. I am confident as I make this prayer of consecration to you, the Queen of Heaven, Our Lady of Champion, in the name of Jesus, our Lord and Savior, Amen.

Prayer for Mary's Protection

On the night of October 8, 1871, a fire broke out in Peshtigo, Wisconsin, and spread into the area of the then-Chapel of Our Lady of Good Help. As people stared death in the eye, they flocked to the place of Mary's apparition, confident in her intercession. Mary protected the land, and the fire passed over the property.

Dear Blessed Mother, your prayers provide protection to those who call upon you. Just as the local townspeople sought refuge at the shrine and you heard their prayers, I ask you to provide your maternal protection over me. Protect me from the evil one and squash his ugly head with your foot. Protect me from all danger and all doubt. Protect me at the hour of my death. May your prayers also protect my family, keeping them safe and faithful; protect my country from all violence and war, and protect our world. Obtain from your Son many graces for all those for whom I pray. I make my prayer through Christ our Lord. Amen.

Prayer for One's Vocation

Sister Adele struggled to know what God wanted her to do. After seeking the advice of a priest in her homeland, she joined her family and immigrated to the United States. Through Mary's apparition, Adele received the revelation of her vocation.

Dear Lord, I wish to serve you and to do what you will for my life. Reveal to me your plans and give me the grace to respond and persevere. Send me holy priests and advisors who will help me discern my vocation. Whatever you ask, may I do it, responding like the Queen of Heaven did, "Behold I am the handmaid of the Lord, be it done unto me according your word."

Healing Prayers

Refer to the Novena for Healing. Any of those prayers could be said apart from the novena.

Prayer for Conversion

Refer to the Novena for Conversion. Any of those prayers could be said apart from the novena.

Prayer for Children

Dear Lord, you entrusted Adele with a mission of teaching the children the faith. Bless the children of my family, my parish, and all the children of the world. Guard their souls against all evil. Sanctify their families. Inspire their teachers. Grant to all children a desire to know you, to love you, and serve you. Through Christ our Lord. Amen.

Prayer for Increased Faith

During the third apparition, Our Lady commended the faith of Adele's companions: "Blessed are they who believe without seeing."

Lord, I profess and renew my faith in you. I believe that you are going to do amazing things in my life, that you will use me to accomplish your will. Renew my faith and deepen my trust in you.

I believe that you exist. When I doubt, help my unbelief.

I believe that you love me.

I believe that Jesus saved me from death.

I believe in the forgiveness of sins.

I believe in the Holy Eucharist, that Christ instituted on the night of the Last Supper, taking bread and wine and saying this is my body, this is my blood.

I believe that Jesus rose from the dead.

I believe that the Holy Spirit is alive in His Church.

I believe in healing and that God continues to heal today.

I believe in heaven and that the saints and my family who have gone before me pray for me.

I believe that God hears my prayers and I believe in the efficacy of the sacraments.

In times of doubt, confusion, trial, sickness, and persecution, increase my faith in you, O Lord.

Help me to believe in the things that I cannot see. And one day, may you confirm these beliefs, when I am able to gaze upon your face and make my home forever in heaven. Amen.

Prayer to Remain Faithful

Dear Lord, your servant Adele remained faithful to God and the Church even amidst trials and difficulties. When I am tempted to abandon my faith and belief in God because of the circumstances of life, trouble in the Church, or persecution by others, help me never to doubt you or abandon my faith. I place my hope and trust in you and your plan for my life. Through Christ our Lord. Amen.

Praying at the National Shrine

When you set foot on the grounds of the National Shrine of Our Lady of Champion, you encounter a peaceful and quaint shrine. The grounds are rather simple, yet profoundly rich for our meditation. While you are at the National Shrine, there are many places you may wish to pray. Explore the outdoor grounds and visit the grottos. Pray in the church and in the oratory below the church. Pray at Sister Adele's grave. The following prayers can help to enrich your experience at each location.

Prayer Before a Pilgrimage

Dear Lord, as I set out on a pilgrimage of faith and devotion to the National Shrine of Our Lady of Champion, I ask that you open my mind and heart to receive the graces you wish to give me. As I travel to the shrine, I carry with me the following petition (name them). Look upon my devotion, prayer, and sacrifice favorably, and receive them as an act of love. Allow me to reach the shrine safely so that I might give you glory and praise. Amen.

St. Francis Grotto

O God, we thank you for the life and legacy of St. Francis of Assisi. His teaching and poverty attracted many to follow his spirituality and way of life, including Adele who founded a tertiary group of Franciscan sisters. We thank you also for the Sisters of St. Francis of the Holy Cross who served at the shrine for many years. St. Francis, please pray for our world, that we might be instruments of peace, and foster a deep respect for creation. Please intercede also for the Church, that young people will still respond to the call of a religious vocation. Help us to embrace the cross as you did. We ask this through Christ our Lord. Amen.

Our Lady of Lourdes of Grotto

Mary, our mother, a year before you appeared to Adele, you visited St. Bernadette Soubirous in Lourdes and became her teacher. You taught her that you were the Immaculate Conception. You prayed with her and prepared her for her First Holy Communion. You also revealed a miraculous spring of healing water. Our Lady of Lourdes, pray for me now, for the healing that I need, for the healing of my family and friends, and for the healing of the world. Though I am far away from the Grotto of Massabielles, I spiritually visit that holy place. Look upon me with love and kindness, a pilgrim here at your grotto. May the graces God wishes to dispense for me flow like a healing river into my life and soul. Thank you for praying for me to Jesus, your Son.

Military Grotto

As I visit this grotto dedicated to the military, I pray for all those who serve our country, defending our freedom. Our Lady of Grace, obtain for the world conversion of heart so that war will never be necessary and the grace of peace may find its place in our country and world. St. Michael, defend us against the evil of the world and cast the fallen angel of hatred and division into the fires of the netherworld. I make my prayer in the holy name of Jesus. Amen.

Sacred Heart of Jesus

O Jesus, I look at your heart, aflame with love for the world and for me. I entrust to your Sacred Heart all my intentions, especially (name intention). I offer my prayers and sacrifices as reparation for my sins and those of the world, which offend your Sacred Heart. Enflame my heart with your love so that I might love everyone with your love. Amen.

Fatima Grotto

Dear Lady of Fatima, thank you for appearing to the children Lucia, Francisco, and Jacinta. I recall your message of praying for peace in the world through the Rosary, praying for conversion, and offering reparation through our sacrifices. As I visit this place where you appeared to Adele, just as you did to the three shepherd children, I renew my commitment to fulfilling your requests, made at Champion and Fatima. May your apparition in Fatima always remind me of the Rosary's importance so that there will never be a day that passes that I neglect this prayer. Obtain from your Son peace for the world, peace in my family, and in my heart. Jesus, please grant me my desires and receive my offering. Amen.

St. John Vianney

Here I stand, before the statue of St. John Vianney, the patron of priests, and I invoke your intercession for all the priests in my life. You were the saintly priest of Ars, dedicated to your people, especially by hearing their confessions. O Lord, I thank you for the priest who baptized me, cleansing me of original sin and claiming me as a child of God. I thank you for the priests who have absolved me of my sins, restoring me to friendship with God. I thank you for the priests who have celebrated the Mass so I could receive the Holy Eucharist. For the priests whose homilies I've heard, who have given me counsel, I thank you O Lord, and I entrust them to the intercession of St. John Vianney. By his prayers and your grace, Almighty God, continue to provide saintly priests for your Church so that I too can become a saint with their help. Finally, I thank you for the priests who guided Adele throughout her life so that she could carry out God's will. Give us holy priests after the example of St. John Vianney, devoted to Christ, His

Church, and the Blessed Mother, through Christ our Lord. Amen.

Pieta

O Mary, I cannot fathom what it must have been like for you to hold the lifeless body of Jesus. You are the sorrowful mother, mourning over the death of Jesus. I realize that each sin I commit was the reason Jesus died on the cross, and causes you to mourn for me, because Jesus proclaimed you mother of all from the cross. Be a mother to me; pray for me that I may not cause you any further anguish. And one day, may you embrace me in the kingdom of heaven, just as you held your Son here on earth. Amen.

Sister Adele's Grave

Dear Lord, I thank you for the life of your servant Adele, who sought to do your will all her days. You sent the Blessed Mother to appear to her and called her to a missionary vocation of prayer and catechesis. Her prayers and teaching converted many souls and her story continues to do so today. We ask you, Almighty God, to grant her the reward of her labors, and give her a home among the saints in the kingdom of heaven. Eternal rest grant unto her, O Lord, and let perpetual light shine upon her. May her soul, and the souls of all the faithful departed, through the mercy of God, rest in peace. Amen.

Apparition Oratory

The Apparition Oratory is a special place of prayer at the National Shrine of Our Lady of Champion. For decades, people have offered their prayers to the Queen of Heaven, lighting votive candles, believing this to be the preserved site of the apparition. Many describe the peaceful atmosphere they experience while praying before the statue of Our Lady of Grace.

A Prayer Before the Statue in the Apparition Oratory

Blessed Mother, I have come here as your pilgrim. When you appeared to Adele you made this place holy, sanctified by your presence among us. I come here just as the pilgrims did in years gone by. I see the crutches they left behind. I hear the stories of grace and favors received. I come here mindful of my own needs and those of others. I lay these petitions down at your feet (name your intentions, speaking from your heart). I know that you have presented these petitions before the throne of your Son. Help me to be open to God's will. As I feel the peace of this place, pray for me, that this peace will remain with me, so that I no longer will fear the future, but trust in God's providence.

Her eyes

Mary, turn your gaze toward me in this moment as I come to you with my petitions. Turn your eyes of mercy toward me and present my petitions (state your intention) to your Son. Your eyes saw the need of the couple at Cana; notice now all that I need, those things that I already know, and those which are not known to me. Look upon me, the sinner that I am, and present me and my prayers to God Most High.

Her smile

Mary, as I kneel before you, I see your smile. Pray for me that I may always live as a noble (son or daughter) of yours, worthy of the kingdom of heaven. Please rejoice with me over the graces which your Son chooses to dispense through your immaculate hands to me, the sinner that I am. I salute you as the cause of our joy. May you not only cause me joy, but may I become the joy of your smile.

Her hands

Into your hands, I place mine. Just as a child holds the hand of his or her mother, I ask you to hold my hand. Guide me through the troubles of life, and always lead me to your son, Jesus. As I place my hands in yours, I know that it is from your hands that God chooses to dispense grace to the world. Please obtain for me the graces I need to live a life worthy of heaven.

Her cincture

Mary, around your waist is a cincture. As you wear this sash, may it be a witness to me of your chastity and purity. Place your cincture of purity around me that I may never displease God with sins of impurity.

Her foot, crushing evil

It was prophesied that your foot would crush the head of the serpent. The devil lurks in the world, looks to snatch our souls from the hands of your Son. Please crush the rearing head of the enemy, especially in regard to this sin (name sin). Obtain for me victory in temptation and perseverance in the grace of God.

Her crown

O Mary, you received the imperishable crown of your Son and have become the Queen of Heaven. As your devoted child, I claim you now to be the Queen of my life and the Queen of my family. Because you are my queen, I trust most that you are my devoted advocate and intercessor.

Her mantle

Clothed with your beautiful mantle, I ask that you wrap your mantle of love and protection around me, that under your mantle I may always find safety and happiness.

Prayer for Lighting a Candle

I stand here, in this place, where many before me have come to pray and entrust their petitions to the maternal intercession of Mary. I stand here, knowing that many pilgrims will come to this sacred place after me, and if God wills it, may I return here to pray again and to give thanks to God for answered prayers. As I go forth from this apparition site, I light this candle and ask Mary to join her prayers to mine, especially for (state intention). This candle is a reminder, that my prayer continues after I leave this place. Thank you, Mary, for praying with me and for my intention, and thank you, God, for the way in which you will answer my prayer according to your providence. Open my heart to accept your will and give me confidence in heaven's prayers, through Christ our Lord. Amen.

Prayer After a Pilgrimage

Thank you, Jesus, for the ways which you are alive and at work in my life. (*Feel free to name anything for which you wish to thank God.*) Thank you for the time I was able to spend with your mother, and for the prayers she offers to you. As I leave the shrine, help me to be open to God's will in all things. And as I see His will at play in the world, may I always be moved to give thanks to God. Thank you for this special time of prayer and pilgrimage, and if it be in accord with your will, call me back to this shrine again, but if not, I look forward to one day seeing the Lady whom Adele saw, and the Lord whom I have served throughout my life in the life that knows no end.

Appendix

The Original Devotion to Notre Dame de Bon Secours

Mary has many names, or shall we call them titles? The Litany of Loreto refers to many different titles of Mary, but not all of them. Some of her titles refer to a city name corresponding to an apparition location; for example, Our Lady of Lourdes or Our Lady of Fatima. There are also devotional titles of Our Lady such as *Our Lady, Undoer (or Untier) of Knots.* And then there are many variations of titles which all have a unique history. One such devotion is to Mary under the title of Our Lady of Good Help.

Each year pilgrims from around the world visit the first and only approved Marian apparition site in the United States of America located in Champion, Wisconsin (close to Green Bay). Pilgrims arrive at the National Shrine of Our Lady of Champion and learn the story of Mary's apparition to Adele Brise, a twenty-eight-year-old Belgian immigrant, who the Queen of Heaven visited three times, speaking only once, on October 9, 1859. Mary asked Adele to offer her Holy Communion for the conversion of sinners, make a general confession, and gather the children in the area and teach them what they needed to know for salvation.

I've reflected at great lengths on the Wisconsin apparition, writing about its theological, spiritual, and pastoral implications, and I speak about the apparition often at conferences and gatherings. In my conversations, I often hear people refer to the National Shrine as "Our Lady of Good Health," "Our Lady of Good Hope," "Our Lady Help of Christians," and "Our Lady of Perpetual Help," to name only a few.

However, to be precise, the National Shrine welcoming pilgrims to commemorate the 1859 Wisconsin apparition was dedicated to Our Lady of Good Help, but I can understand the confusion. The title Our Lady of Good Help is rather obscure, and not common in the United States; the title's historical roots lie in France, Belgium, and Canada. Since Adele came from Belgium, she had a devotion to Our Lady under this title and asked for the chapel to be dedicated to Notre Dame de Bon Secours (Our Lady of Good Help). This is the reason why it was called the National Shrine of Our Lady of Good Help instead of the title by which Mary revealed herself to Adele as the Queen of Heaven, or even by the geographic location (Our Lady of Champion). This has since been rectified with the name change to Our Lady of Champion. Further confusion occurs, especially among Wisconsinites, with some calling it "Our Lady of Good Hope" because in Milwaukee, a popular exit is called Good Hope Road, which also has a church dedicated to that title of Mary.

When it comes to Mary's many titles, a lot of them use the adjective *good* or refer to her help. Each title of Mary is unique and has its own history. None of the devotions are the same. To distinguish these titles of Mary, I offer a brief snippet of the historical origin of each title, thereby making clear the history of Our Lady of Good Help as set apart from the other various "good" and "helping" titles of Mary.

Our Lady of Good Health: A title associated with a Marian apparition to a young boy in the sixteenth or seventeenth century in Velankanni, India. Beyond the apparition, perhaps people called upon Mary with this title asking her to intercede in times of sickness.

Our Lady of Good Hope: The nineteenth-century apparitions of Mary in Pontmain, France are known as Our Lady of Hope, but not Good Hope. A devotion to Mary exists under the title "Nuestra Senora Esperanza" and is oftentimes modified with the word "buena," translating to Our Lady of Good Hope. The Spanish devotion centers around the Virgin Mary and the Advent season, in which the Christian people are given hope by the birth of the Savior. As mentioned earlier, this is also the name of a parish in Milwaukee, Wisconsin located on Good Hope Road.

Our Lady of Good Counsel: The image of Our Lady of Good Counsel is often associated with some book covers of St. Louis de Montfort's *True Devotion to Mary*. The image of Mary miraculously appeared in a Genazzano church in 1467.

Our Lady of Good Success: A title of Mary rooted in two different cultures. The first dates to the 1400s in Belgium where a statue from Scotland (formerly called Our Lady of Aberdeen) quickly became known as Our Lady of Good Success, winning the conversion of Calvinists to Catholicism. A second emergence of Our Lady of Good Success arises out of Ecuador in the late 1500s and early 1600s following apparitions of Mary received by a Conceptionist nun named Mother Mariana. People devoted to Our Lady of Good Success have suggested remarkable similarities between the words Mary spoke then and our culture today.

Our Lady, Help of Christians: The National Shrine of Our Lady of Champion was not the only National Shrine in the Wisconsin dedicated to a helping title of Mary. The Carmelite friars at Holy Hill serve the National Shrine of Mary, Help of Christians in Hubertus, Wisconsin. Historically this title of Mary was promoted by St. John Bosco and the Salesian order. The title dates back as far as St. John Chrysostom, and spread during the time in which Our Lady's assistance was invoked by Christians during war. St. John Bosco constructed a basilica in Turin to Mary under this title.

Our Lady (or Mother) of Perpetual Help: This title of Mary is associated with one of the most popular icons of Mary, in which two angels hover around Mary and the Christ-child with the instruments of the Passion. The icon hung in various churches over the years and today the Redemptorist order promotes this devotion and has custody of the Church in which the icon is enshrined. The image has been venerated by countless pilgrims and has also received the attention of many popes throughout history.

Our Lady of Prompt Succor: A title of Mary associated with the Ursuline order and venerated by Catholics in New Orleans. Today her intercession is invoked against storms. The intercession of Our Lady of Prompt Succor is credited with the victory of the Battle of New Orleans.

Who Is Our Lady of Good Help?

Sanctuaries to Notre Dame de Bon Secours can be traced back as early as the eleventh century by oral tradition, or to the thirteenth century in the historical record. The popularization of this title arises out of Mary's assistance to those who call upon her, especially in 1477 when the Duke of Lorraine, Rene II, defeated Charles the Bold, Duke of Burgundy, during the Battle of Nancy. In Nancy, France, this victory prompted the building of a chapel to Our Lady of Good Help.

Devotion to Our Lady of Good Help exists principally in France and Belgium but made its way to North America, to Canada, and the United States. In France, there are at least four basilicas, six churches, and seven chapels dedicated to this title of Mary. Within the devotional cult to Bon Secours, we find the origin of the pilgrimage church, accompanied by the prayers and hymns pilgrims recited and sang. And each devotional center possesses a statue of Mary, niched away in a quiet place of prayer for the pilgrims who seek Mary's intercession. Presumably, from France, the chapel dedicated to Our Lady of Good Help in Montreal, founded by St. Marguerite Bourgeoys in 1657, takes its inspiration.

The Belgian people also honor Mary under this title. In Belgium, the principal site of devotion dates to 1637 with a basilica constructed on the location of "Mary between two oak trees" in Peruwelz. Adele Brise, the Wisconsin visionary, born in the province of Brabant (Dion le Val), in Belgium, lived approximately 100 kilometers from Peruwelz. There are, at least, two other churches to Bon Secours in Belgium, in Zetrund-Lumay (22 km) and Brussels (39 km). In the Church of St. Steven, in Ohain, 20 kilometers from Dion le Val, the faithful venerate a statue of Bon Secours from the 1700s. We know from the chapel's commemorating the apparitions received by Brise that she herself had a devotion to Mary under this title. Around Dion le Val, the Belgian people erected roadside chapels to house a statue of the Madonna. Passersby would stop and pray briefly in front of the image. Wherever they went, on the street corners or in the fields, they would find the Bon Secours and offer an Ave.

The cult of Our Lady of Good Help originating in Europe called upon Mary for help during times of turmoil especially during revolutions, wars, plagues, and pestilence. In the organic development of the devotion, it took on a unique maritime aspect. The devotion to Our Lady of Good Help existed long before the 1859 apparitions received by Brise, in which Mary does not reveal herself as the Lady of Good Help, but instead as the Queen of Heaven.[107] The only semblance of help, spoken of by the Queen of Heaven, were her parting words, "Go, and fear nothing, I will help you." Adele relied on the intercession of Mary through-

---

107 It is the opinion of this author that language referring to the apparition of Our Lady of Good Help or the message of Our Lady of Good Help is errant and should be avoided. While Our Lady of Good Help is Mary of Nazareth, who is the Queen of Heaven, the chosen name of Mary revealed to Adele (Queen of Heaven) has theological significance and should be honored.

out her years of service in the Lord's vineyard. This help came through answered prayers when food or money was needed and just happened to show up. Locals received help on the night of October 8, 1871, when a fire threatened the area of the chapel, and people flocked there seeking Mary's help. The property was spared and lives were saved, all this being realized on the morning of the twelfth anniversary of Mary's apparition. To this day, pilgrims receive help from Mary as they seek her intercession for miracles in their lives.

Conclusion

Each title of Mary with reference to its modifier, "good," or the "help" Mary provides, has a unique history, and each devotion is different. All these titles of Mary might leave her devotees confused, especially when you talk about Perpetual Help, Good Hope, Good Health, and Good Help, among others. Mary surely is the Help of Christians; she promptly assists her children, and her help is perpetual, but in Wisconsin, at the site commemorating the 1859 Marian apparition of the Queen of Heaven, she was formerly called Our Lady of Good Help.

Timeline of the Historical Devotion to Our Lady of Good Help

(N.D. Bon Secours)

Eleventh Century: Basilique Notre Dame de Bon Secours, Rouen, France -- While written documents do not assert this, the living history and tradition of this community asserts that devotion to Our Lady of Good Help existed since the eleventh century, and a sanctuary existed there in 1034. Travelers by boat along the Seine made pilgrimage there, and a number of model ships were left suspended as a sign of their devotion. In 1552, over 50,000 people gathered at the basilica on pilgrimage.

Thirteenth Century: Basilique Notre Dame de Bon Secours, Guingamp, France -- The church dates to the eleventh century, but devotion to

NDBS begins sometime in the thirteenth century. The basilica gained prominence especially during times of war. In 1448, Pope Nicholas V granted an indulgence to those who visited the basilica on the feast of Mary's nativity. The image of NDBS was crowned in 1857 by order of Pius IX and in 1899 the shrine became a basilica.

1443: Chapelle Notre Dame de Bon Secours, Nantes -- Along the bank of the Loire, a primitive chapel to NDBS was built in 1443. Given the proximity to water, this chapel was known for Mary's protection of travelers, help of those in danger, guardian of the besieged city, and defender against the heresies of Protestantism and Jansenism.

1477: Notre Dame de Bon Secours, Nancy, France -- This basilica of Bon Secours rises out of one of the momentous events of French history, the victory which saved Nancy and the country. The title of NDBS was popularized in Lorraine by the Duke of Lorraine, Rene II, following the defeat of Charles the Temeraire on January 5, 1477 after the Battle of Jarville. In remembrance of Our Lady's help—that is, her good help—the Duke of Lorraine built a chapel in 1494 near the battle cemetery. In 1630, during a time of war, famine, and pestilence, the people vowed to offer Mass weekly in honor of the Mother of God. To memorialize this, an altar was erected in 1645.

Sixteenth Century: Basilique Notre Dame de Bon-Secours, Saint Avold, France -- Two legends tell of the decision to build a chapel in this location. The first legend says a man carried a statue of Mary and after resting for a while could not lift the statue; others helped to lift, but they still could not. A chapel was thus built. The second legend tells that Benedictine monks, while travelling along the path of Valmont, caught sight of a statue of Mary in a bush, but it quickly vanished. Later, they saw it a second time, and a decision was made to build a chapel at the location. In 1793, the chapel was destroyed by the Jacobins but the statue survived the Revolution. The cult of NDBS was restored in 1802, and pilgrimages began in the nineteenth century. Pilgrimages were encouraged in the 1890s and the feast day was celebrated on May 24.

1637: Basilique Notre Dame de Bon Secours, Peruwelz, Belgium -- This basilica was built where a tree housing a statue of the Virgin with Child was venerated. People invoked Mary's intercession because of the plague. Pilgrimages continued throughout the years, even during the wars of Louis XIV and during the Revolution of 1789.

1641: Basilique Notre Dame de Bon Secours, Lablachere (Vivrais), France -- According to legend a doctor, while traveling to see a patient, fell underneath his horse and was caught in the stirrups. Realizing his only hope was in God and the prayers of the Virgin, he promised to build a chapel to honor Mary in this location, if his life was spared. Forgetting his promise, he passed by the same area, and again experienced trouble with his horse. He renewed his vow and promised to build a chapel to Our Lady. The chapel was dedicated to Our Lady of Good Help, and many miracles were reported through Our Lady's intercession.

1657: Chapel of Notre Dame de Bon Secours, Montreal Canada -- St. Marguerite Bourgeoys built the first chapel to Notre Dame de Bon Secours, a small stone chapel. The Jesuit missionary, Claude Pijart, selected the name of the chapel, NDBS. In 1672, Bourgeoys received the oak statuette venerated at the chapel from Baron de Fancamp. Bishop

Bourget, in 1847 and 1848, amidst a health epidemic of typhus and Asiatic cholera, issued favorable pastoral documents, renewing pilgrimages to the chapel, calling upon Mary's assistance. He established a confraternity and May 24 as the feast day. Today, replicas of boats hang from the ceiling, in gratitude for safe voyage along the St. Lawrence Seaway.

1817: Notre Dame de Bon Secours, Puivert, France -- While devotion to NDBS goes back many centuries, the sanctuary in Puivert was built rather recently in 1817, located near the lakeshore. Pilgrimages became popular in the 1900s and were accompanied by specific prayers and hymns to Our Lady of Good Help.

1876: Chapelle Notre Dame de Bon Secours, Dieppe, France -- Faces toward the sea with a silhouette of a lighthouse. Travelers along the sea look to the Bon Secours for safe harbor and "bon voyage" (safe travels). It was consecrated in 1876 and served as a place of pilgrimage. It is a principal place of worship for sailors and contains a memorial to those who drowned at sea.

Prayers to Our Lady of Good Help

Blessed Virgin Mary, Our Lady of Good Help, by you, the son of God became our brother. You are the Mother of God, Queen of Heaven and you are Mother to all. See our dead, our sick, and all who suffer from violence, hunger and poverty. Be for all the Good Help and give them more docile hearts to the Holy Spirit, more fraternal and more daring. Make us all together sowers of hope, and courageous witnesses of your Son, Jesus Christ our Lord. Amen.

Peruwelz, Belgium

Prayer to Our Lady of Good Help

Our Lady of Good Help, O you whose name signifies kindness and inspires trust, here I am at your feet to request the good help that you grant to those who pray to you.

This good help I await, O Mary, during my life; be my star in the night here below, my rest from labor, my refuge from danger, my support in virtue, my strength in struggle, my peace in adversity, my comfort in suffering.

I await it most especially, O Mary, at the hour of my death; be with me at that ultimate moment to welcome my sinful soul, present it yourself to its Judge and guide it into heaven.

Our Lady of Good Help, I put all of my interests in you for all time and eternity: I loyally surrender myself to your motherly heart.

Prayer to Our Lady of Good Help

O you who for so many centuries overwhelm us, who call on you by the name Our Lady of Good Help, with many favors, we kneel at your feet with confidence. Receive us with kindness, we who always call you mother, protect us, protect our children, bless our families. You, the health of the sick, comforter of the afflicted, calm our sorrows, wipe our tears. You, the guardian of innocence, the refuge of sinners, save us from sin, remind us of our distractions. You, the support of the dying, the hope of those who suffer in purgatory, pray for us at the hour of our death and open the door of heaven. Amen.

Rouen, France

Prayer to Our Lady of Good Help

O most holy and august Virgin Mary, Mother of God, Our Lady of Good Help, never has it been said that anyone who, in abundant confidence, holy and resolute, has begged your protection and been forsaken. Enlivened with such confidence, I have recourse to you, O most holy Mother, O most perfect of creatures! Never has the stain of sin soiled your soul: like your Son, you are full of kindness, even for great sinners who are truly penitent, or at least sincerely long for conversion. O Mother of Mercy, please deign to take an interest in me; you know my miseries, my weaknesses, and all my needs; hasten to my aid. You are the Queen of the heavens, angels, and saints; you can do anything through Jesus Christ your Son; you have some of His almighty power; you are the channel of His grace and favor, be my powerful mediator with Him; be so kind as to obtain from Him all the spiritual and temporal aid necessary to sustain me in the midst of the pitfalls that surround me.

You are the consoler of the afflicted, please give me grace from God to cope with my troubles, all the pains of this life, with that patience and acceptance you demonstrated to me on earth as an example, in order that, through my submission, I may deserve, as you do, to enjoy eternal consolation.

You are the refuge of the sinner; please give me true contrition, forgiveness for my faults, and the grace to avoid sin.

Finally, you are the help, support, and advocate of the faithful who invoke you in holy dispositions. Prostrate at your feet, I beg for your kindness; please grant my prayer. If you protect me, I have nothing to fear, not from the enemy of my salvation because you are more powerful than hell; not from my Judge because a single prayer from you can calm Him. Therefore, pray for me to Jesus, your dear Son; tell Him that you protect me, and He will have mercy upon me. O my Mother, my protector and patron saint, I throw myself into your merciful arms, I fully entrust myself to your

Good Help: it is in this confidence that I live and die. Amen.

Bon Secours Prayer Manual, Nancy, France

Prayer to Our Lady of Bon-Secours

Mary, Our Lady of Good Help, Jesus your son has assured me that you are also my Mother. With you, I come to praise and thank our God.

You taught Jesus to pray; teach me too. You hurried in joy toward Elizabeth; help me reach out to others with the same love. You interceded at Cana; teach me to do all that Jesus tells me. You suffered with your Son; stay with me always. You were present with the apostles at Pentecost; be with us in the Church today.

Mary, Our Lady of Good Help, keep us close to you, obtain for us steadfast faith, unfailing hope, and a love that knows no measure. Amen.

Montreal, Canada

Litany of Our Lady of Good Help

Puivert, France

Lord, have mercy on us.
Christ, have mercy on us.
Lord, have mercy on us.
Jesus Christ, listen to us. Jesus Christ, hear us.
Our heavenly Father, who is God, have mercy on us.
Son, redeemer of the world, who is God, have mercy on us.
Holy Spirit, who is God, have mercy on us.
Holy Trinity, who is one God, have mercy on us.
Our Lady Help of Christians, pray for us.
Our Lady Help of the Holy Church and of the sovereign pontiff during the persecutions, pray for us.
Our Lady Help of all the pastors of souls in the fulfillment of their ministries, pray for us.
Our Lady Help of missionaries in the desert, pray for us.
Our Lady Help of kings and magistrates in difficult circumstances, pray for us.
Our Lady Help against the dangers of war, pray for us.
Our Lady Help of the people who long for peace, pray for us.

Our Lady Help of the soldier who invokes you, pray for us.

Our Lady Help of virtuous mothers at the birth of their infants, pray for us.

Our Lady Help of abandoned children and of small orphans, pray for us.

Our Lady Help of young Catholics against the seductions of the world, pray for us.

Our Lady Help of souls against temptations, pray for us.

Our Lady Help of sinners who return to God, pray for us.

Our Lady Help of the persecuted, pray for us.

Our Lady Help of the prisoners, pray for us.

Our Lady Help of navigators during shipwrecks, pray for us.

Our Lady Help of widows, the feeble, and the poor, pray for us.

Our Lady Help and healing of the sick, pray for us.

Our Lady Help against the drought, pray for us.

Our Lady Help against fires, pray for us.

Our Lady Help against floods, pray for us.

Our Lady Help powerfully at the hour of death, pray for us.

Our Lady Help of the souls in purgatory, pray for us.

From the heights of heaven, help us Mary.
When the gates of hell are unleashed against the Holy Church, help us Mary.
When Satan and the world besiege us, help us Mary.
When the war, the plague, and famine overwhelm us, help us Mary.
When the weather threatens us, help us Mary.
When misfortunes and disease fall upon us, help us Mary.
When the wicked persecute us, help us Mary.
When our friends abandon us, help us Mary.
When we call upon you in time of need, help us Mary.
When our last hour strikes, help us Mary.
When our trembling soul leaves this world, help us Mary.
When the doors of eternity will open before us, help us Mary.
Lamb of God, who takes away the sins of the world, pardon us, Lord.

Lamb of God, who takes away the sins of the world, hear us, Lord.
Lamb of God, who takes away the sins of the world, have mercy on us, Lord.

Jesus listen to us, Jesus hear us.
Pray for us, Holy Mother of God.
That we may be made worthy of the promises of Christ.

Let us pray. We appeal to your holy protection, holy Mother of God, Our Lady of Good Help, listen favorably the prayers which we offer in our need, deliver us from the perils of our environment, O Virgin filled with glory and blessing. Amen.

Hymns to Our Lady of Good Help

The Ave of Our Lady of Good Help

Melody of the Ave of Lourdes

Refrain: Ave, Ave, Ave Maria (repeat).

Blessed sanctuary
So dear to our hearts,
From the good Mother
Sing the favors.

O Virgin Mary,
You choose these places;
To the soul who prays You show the heavens.

Your gracious image
Was the subject of a vow,
And bears witness,

To the love of a God.

When the deep sea
Unleashes waves,
You appeared on the wave
Beside the sailors.

Your hand, O Mary,
Snatches from death
The sailor who prays,
Brings him to port.

With enthusiasm
Puivert received you,
Made in your tenderness
Looking for salvation.

You saw the misery
Of your beloved people,
By you, good Mary,
Were we delivered.

The terrible plague
Retreats suddenly;
Is it not visible,
Your intercessory power!

Though this chapel Is then evident
A faithful love
That still remains for you.
More verses not included.

Puivert, France

We Have Recourse as in Bygone Days

We have recourse, as in bygone days,
To you, Our Lady of Good Help.
Protect Puivert and its surroundings,
Over us watch, watch always.

Puivert honors you,
And all its hope, Guardian Virgin,
Is in your power.

Here, all ages,
With resounding love,
Offer you their homages,
Their well wishes and their songs.

Through you, good Mother,
The poor soul afflicted

With troubles hopes
For relief.

To the sick once more
You give health;
He who beseeches you
Is quickly answered.

Through you hope
Returns to the sinner,
And your clemency
Soothes his heart.

To you the Holy Father
Always has recourse,
O tender Mother,
Please help him always.

To our country
Keep the faith;
Jesus will be Our king for life.

Puivert, France

A Hymn to Our Lady of Good Help

Our Lady of Good Help,
Your name for my tender soul
Is the echo of my heavenly home.
It is my joy during my somber days.

Our Lady of Good Help,
Your name has dried many a tear,
And when the time of alarm comes,
To you alone does man have recourse.

Our Lady of Good Help,
To you the children and mothers
Will offer tears and prayers,
And you always comfort them.

Our Lady of Good Help,
Your name is a name of hope,
Through you suffering is less harsh
And through you our burdens are less heavy.

Our Lady of Good Help,
When the stormy winds blow,
Raising their dreadful heads toward Heaven,
The sailors cry out to you: help us.

Our Lady of Good Help,
When I fear my weakness,
When pain wounds my heart,
It is to you, Mother, that I turn.

Our Lady of Good Help,
When my final hour arrives,
Open to me the holy home
Where we will love God always.

Rouen, France

Acknowledgments

The year was most likely 2002. The pastor of my home parish, Fr. Dave Ruby, arranged for a local pilgrimage to a few sites in my diocese: the newly built Carmelite monastery, the Shrine of St. Joseph at St. Norbert Abbey (now located at St. Norbert College), and the Shrine of Our Lady of Champion. That was the first time I visited the site of Mary's appearance in Champion, Wisconsin, but it would not be the last, as I would return there on August 15, 2005 for the Assumption Holy Day, and hundreds of times since. It was the beginning of my lifelong devotion to the Blessed Mother.

My fondness for Marian apparitions began when I was a young boy. In my hometown there was a lady who organized pilgrimages throughout the world to places where Mary had appeared or was believed to have been appearing. The stories she would share about these apparitions and messages of Mary mesmerized me. And in 2005, she brought me with her on one of those pilgrimages.

That ignited my Marian fervor which has led me to visit the most popular sites of Mary's appearances. May God grant Joyce Lightner eternal rest.

I am grateful to my bishop, Bishop David Ricken, who launched a commission to approve the 1859 Marian apparition, declaring it worthy of belief on December 8, 2010. With such an announcement, and the influx of pilgrims, help was needed there during the summer of 2011. In May of 2011, I presented a theological analysis of Mary's message at the annual meeting of the Mariological Society of America. Given my background researching the apparition, I was asked to assist during those first months of summer pilgrimage post-approval.

I am indebted to Mundelein Seminary, which awarded me the Monsignor John Canary Grant in 2014 so I could do further research on the historical devotion to Our Lady under the title Our Lady of Good Help. Their grant funded my trips to Belgium, France, and Canada in order to study the history and encounter the devotion.

The Marian Library, located at the University of Dayton, is home to the largest collection of books on the Blessed Virgin. Their library provided me the resources I needed to find more of the prayers and history of devotion to Our Lady of Good Help. Dr. Gloria Falcão Dodd provided immense help during my research visit.

My author friend, Susan Tassone, often provides helpful insights, especially when I am stumped and reach out for counsel. The same is true for Mary Anne Urlakis. Their feedback on a few of the prayers was critical in bringing forth the best pilgrim manual possible.

I am grateful to Jefferey Campbell, owner of Vesuvius Press, who in May of 2012 took me on as a fledgling author at the age of twenty-three. Some of the devotions contained within this prayer manual were originally published with some of his imprints before he decided to return to his publishing roots of publishing only topics of Franciscan spirituality.

In August 2018, I spoke at the Catholic Marketing Network conference. It was there that I met Conor Gallagher and John Moorehouse from TAN Books. I wanted to meet with them during that visit and pitch this prayer manual, and as I found out, they were interested in having me write for their publishing house. Our interest in one another was mutual from an author/publisher perspective. I am grateful for their patience with me as I juggle my extracurricular writing with my role as administrator of two parishes.

To Columba Publishing and Richard Gibbons, who in 2018 released *The Knock Prayer Book*, which inspired me to compile my devotionals into one book, and served also as the impetus to compose several new devotional prayers.

To those who follow me on social media, especially Twitter; often times I will tweet out questions, looking for some help with my writing. Thank you for replying and providing your thoughts. When I was in need, I also turned to Twitter, and a few people came to assistance. A special word of thanks to Marian Carney for converting the text of a pdf into a word document, allowing me the fortune of not having to re-type a document, and to Sarah Coffey, who helped to copyedit the manuscript before submission to TAN Books.